海外中華古籍書志書目叢刊

加拿大多倫多大學
慕氏藏書目（外一種）

3

加拿大多倫多大學
東亞圖書館　編

喬曉勤　主編

國家圖書館出版社

第三冊目録

The University of Toronto Chinese Library

. . . .

Accession No. 1097   Index No. 031-6 8 9 9

Title 四書便蒙   Ssu Shu Pien Mêng

Classification A 131

Subject The Classic of The Four Books

References

Author Chiao Yüan-hsi 焦袁熹

Edition Li-pen-chai. 5th. year of Tao Kuang
         Pai mien paper

Index

Bound in 2 t'ao, 14 ts'e

Remarks

The University of Toronto Chinese Library

. . . .

103

Accession No. 1098   Index No.   030/ehi

Title   Chü Hua Lu   咀華錄

~~(Literary means "To Chew followers)~~

Classification   D - 53

Subject   A general collection of mandates, memorials, extracts and
letters.

References

凝瑞堂

Author   Compiled by the master of Ning Jui Hall of the Ch'ing

Edition   Preserved in Ning ~~Hai~~ *Jui* Hall

Printed Tao Kwang 20th year

Index   1 t'ao, 4 chuan, 8 t'se, mien Lin paper

Bound in   in perfect condition

Remarks

The University of Toronto Chinese Library

. . . .

Accession No. 1099   Index No. 164/kfbz

Title   醫時天言
         I Shih Liu Yen

Classification   C - 33

Subject   Military strategy

References   Compiled by Wêng Chuan-Chao of the Ch'ing

Author

Edition   Home edition
           printed 20th year of Kwang Hsü

Index   None

Bound in   1 t'ao, 6 chuan, 4 t'si ts'e
            Mien Lien paper

Remarks

The University of Toronto Chinese Library

. . . .

Accession No.   1100 ⁶³   Index No.   085/iii

Title   Hsiang Yen Lu   湘煙錄

Classification   C - 13

Subject   A collection of essays

References

Author   Compiled by Ming Tzu-ching and Liu Chün-pu

Edition   Liu Feng-Sheng Kao, Chia Ch'ing Year
                          -ko

Index   provided

Bound in   1 t'ao, 16 chüan, 6 ts'e, bamboo paper

Remarks

The University of Toronto Chinese Library

. . . .

Accession No. 1101   Index No. 120/cbi

Title Chi Yüan Pien   紀元編   Chi Yuan Pien

Classification   B -157

Subject   Dynastic chronology or record

References

Author Collected and recorded by Liu Sheng-ju of the Ch'ing.   元承衵

Edition   Printed in the year Tao Kwang, Hsin sheng mao, 1831

Index   A brief index provided

Bound in   1 tao, 3 chüan, 4 tse
           "Mao-pien" paper
Remarks

3

The University of Toronto Chinese Library

. . . .

Accession No. 1102   70   Index No. *162-dead*

Title Chin Szu Lu Chi Chieh   近思錄集解

Classification   C - 13

Subject A collection and exposition of the literary works of some
outstanding scholars

References

Author Original compiler, Chu Hsi of the Sung, collected and
朱熹、
interpreted by ~~Yen Tisai~~ *Yeh Ts'ai* 葉采

Edition

Index   provided

Bound in   1 t'ao, 14 chüan, 4 ts'e, Kai-Hua paper

Remarks

The University of Toronto Chinese Library

· ·

Accession No. 1103³³   Index No.   149/obcf

Title   Tu Shih Chi ~~Luch~~ *Liao*   讀史紀畧

Classification   B - 52

Subject   Notes on History

References   清 蕭濬

Author Hsiao Chün of the Ch'ing, *Chien Lung prion*

Edition ~~Chiong~~ ~~Chiu Hsuan~~ *Tan Ching Hsien*
         Bamboo paper

Index   provided

Bound in 1 t'ao, 4 chuan, 4 t'se.

Remarks

The University of Toronto Chinese Library

. . . .

Accession No. 1104 98   Index No. 067/zfbi

Title Wen Chang Kuei Fang 文章軌範

Classification   D - 73

Subject   A collection of standard prose

References

Author   Hsieh Fang-te of the Sung 宋. 謝枋得
          Hsieh

Edition   Not dated

           "mien lien" paper

Index   provided

Bound in   1 t'ao, 7 chüan 2 tu se

Remarks

8

The University of Toronto Chinese Library

. . . .

Accession No. 1105   Index No.   020/cdg↑ g

Title   Pao Hsiao Kung Chou Yi

包 拳 肅 公 奏 議

Classification   B - 72

Subject Memorials of Pao Cheng

References

Author   Composed by Pao Cheng

Edition   not dated, plate preserved by Shang Hsia Ko
          "mien-lien" paper

Index   none

Bound in   1 t'ao, 4 tshe

Remarks

6

The University of Toronto Chinese Library

. . . .

Accession No.   1106   Index No.   075/dhkc

31

Title   Tung Kuan Han Chi   東觀漢紀
                 Kuan

Classification B - 42 別史

Subject   ~~Offical History~~ a record of the Han Dynastry (Later-Han 後漢)

References

Author   Compiled by ~~Han~~ Ming Ti 劉珍撰 according to 隋書經籍志 ~~of the Han~~. 漢明帝

Edition   Wu Ying Tien Chü Cheng Edition

Index   provided

Bound in   1 t'ao, 24 chüan, 8 tsê

Remarks

10

The University of Toronto Chinese Library

. . . .

Accession No. 1107   Index No.   075/ijhg

Title   Chu Shao Chi Yü   楚騷綺語

Classification   C - 13

Subject   The outstanding phrases of the Elegies of Chu

References

Author   Compiled by Chang Chih-hsiang of the Ming   張之象

Edition   Ming, Wan Li, Ping Tzu Year

Index   provided

Bound in   1 t'ao, 6 chüan, 6 ts'e

Remarks

The University of Toronto Chinese Library
....

Accession No. 1108 ²⁹ ⁷

Index No. 018/ecgk

Title   Pieh Chi Pu Yi   別記補遺

Classification   B - 52

Subject   Miscellaneous historical writings

References

Author   Compiled by Hsü Po Ch'u of Ming Dynasty. 明. 徐燉初

Edition   Supplimented by Sung Chueh 宋珏
printed by Sung Ming Tsai

Index   provided

Bound in   1 t'ao, 2 Chuan 2 ts'e

Remarks

12

The University of Toronto Chinese Library

....

Accession No.   1109   Index No.   120/ozl

Title <s>Shu</s> Hsü Wen <s>Hsüan</s> Hsüan   續文選

Classification   D - 73

Subject   A selection of essays and prose

References

Author   Compiled by T'ang Kung Meng of the Ming 明．湯公孟

Edition   Plate of Hsi Kue T'ang Wang-li

Index   provided

Bound in   2 t'ao, 32 chuan, 16 tuše

Remarks

13

The University of Toronto Chinese Library

. . . .

10

<u>Accession No.</u> 1110   <u>Index No.</u> 024/azbf

<u>Title</u> Ch'ien Wen Liu Shu T'ung ~~Yao~~ *yao*

千　文　六　書　統　要

<u>Classification</u>   A - 161

<u>Subject</u>   Graphic dictionaries

<u>References</u>

清，李登

<u>Author</u>   Composed by Li Teng and others of the Ch'ing

<u>Edition</u>   plate by Shih Chu Tsai, K'ang Hsi period

<u>Index</u>   none

<u>Bound in</u>   1 tao, 6 ts'e

<u>Remarks</u>

14

The University of Toronto Chinese Library

. . . .

61

Accession No. 1111   Index No.   042/zjgf

Title   *Hsiao ts'ang* ~~Hsaio Chiang~~ Lang Pi T'ang

小　滄　浪　筆　談

Classification   C - 13

Subject   Poetry and prose rendered in a trip to Hsio Ch'ang Lang

References

阮元

Author   Recorded by Yüan Yüang of the Ch'ing, Chiao Ch'ing year
         Ch'ieh Kiang Chieh Yüan   Bamboo paper
Edition

Index   None.

Bound in   1 tao, 4 chuan, 4 ts'e

Remarks

The University of Toronto Chinese Library

. . . .

Accession No. 1112 [70]   Index No. 140/ofpi

Title   Tu Shu Ts'ung Lu

讀書叢錄

Classification   C - 338

Subject   Collection of reprints

References

Author   Hung Yi Hsüan of the Ch'ing   洪頤煊

Edition   Tao Kwang the 2nd year (1822), Home edition, printed by
          Fu Wen Tsai in Canton

Index   provided

Bound in 1 tao, 24 chuan, 6 ts'e

Remarks

The University of Toronto Chinese Library

. . . .

61

Accession No. 1113   Index No.   181/icgd

Title   Yang Li Shih Ch'eng Chi
         yen
         顏李師承記

Classification   C - 13

Subject   Philosophy and related subjects

References

Author   Hsü Shih Ch'ang   徐世昌

Edition   Home library, not dated

           Mien Lien paper

Index   none

Bound in   1 t'ao, 9 chuan, 3 t'se 2 supplementary t'se

Remarks

The University of Toronto Chinese Library

. . . .

Accession No.   1114   Index No.   075/fghf

Title   T'ung Ying Ch'ing Hua

           桐 陰 清 話

Classification   C - 368

Subject   Miscellanrous narratives, records and sayings

References

Author   I Yun Chü of Ch'ing Dynasty   清、倪雲癯

Edition   T'ung Chih 11th year (1872)

Index   none

Bound in   1 tao, 8 chuan, 4 t'se white paper

Remarks

The University of Toronto Chinese Library

. . . .

Accession No. 1115   Index No.   030/edgg

Title   Shen Yin Yü Chieh Lu

呻 吟 語 節 錄

Classification   C - 13

Subject   Philosophy and Ethics

References

Author   Lu Kun of the Ming   明、呂坤

Edition   T'ung Chih 8th year,   Home library edtion

Index   provided

Bound in   1 tao, 6 chuan, 4 t'se, Mien lien paper

Remarks

The University of Toronto Chinese Library
. . . .

101

Accession No. 1116   Index No. 067-3A

Title   Wen Chi   文集   Tai Shih Yi Shu   戴氏遺書

Classification   D -43

Subject   A collection of prose

References

Author   Tai Cheng of the Ching   戴震

Edition   printed by Wu P'o Hsieh, not dated

Index   none

Bound in   1 t'ao, 10 chuan, 4 t'se, bamboo paper

Remarks

20

The University of Toronto Chinese Library

. . . .

Accession No. 1117   93   Index No. 162/1夌夋 b b

Title Liao Tung San Chia Shih Ch'ao 遼東三家詩鈔

Classification D - 38

Subject A collection of verse

References

Author Compiled by Yüang Ching K'ai 袁金鎧

Edition not dated, preserved by Feng T'ien Hui Kwan

Index None

Bound in 1 t'ao, 4 kinds, 14 chuan, 7 tsê
       Lien Shih paper
Remarks

The University of Toronto Chinese Library

. . . .

Accession No. 1118   Index No. 072/edbh

Title Ch'ing Ch'iu Feng Kuo Tso Chuan

春 秋 方 國 左 傳

Classification   A - 101

Subject   "Ch'un Ch'iu"   Spring and Autumn Annals

References

Author Commented by Lu Yüang Ch'ang of the Ching   清 盧 元 昌

Edition   Plate of Sze Mei Lu

Index   provided

Bound in 1 t'ao, 16 chuan, 6 t'se

Remarks

22

The University of Toronto Chinese Library

....

Accession No.   1119   106   Index No.   061/heck

Title   Hsi Pao Hsüan Yi Shuh San Chung

Classification   D-53

惜抱軒遺書三種

Subject   Tsuan Tze Chang Yi -- Index of Hsi Pao Hsuan and supplement
to Mr. Hsi Pao Hsun's key to letter writing

References

Author   Compiled by Yao Nai of the Ch'ing   姚鼐

Edition   Collected and published by Hsu Shih of T'ung Ch'eng

Index   None

Bound in   1 tao, 11 chuan, 4 tse,   mien lien paper

Remarks

20

Accession No. 1120   61   Index No. 118/zйgj

Title   Chu Yeh T'ing Tsa Chih
竹 葉 亭 雜 誌

Classification   C - 308

Subject   Miscellanous records

References

Author   Yao Yuan Chih of the Ch'ing

Edition   Home library edition, Kwangsu period

Index   simple index only

Bound in 1 t'ao, 8 chuan, 4 t'se, bamboo paper

Remarks

24

The University of Toronto Chinese Library

....

Accession No.   1121   Index No. 030/bchg

Title   Shih Chi Ch'ing Hua Lu

史 記 菁 華 錄

Classification   B - 137

Subject   Historical writings

References

Author Yao Chu T'ien of the Ch'ing 清．姚苧田

Edition   Published by Han Mo Yuan at Canton, 9th year of Kwangsu

Index   provided

Bound in 1 t'ao, 6 chuan, 6 ts'e

Remarks

The University of Toronto Chinese Library

. . . .

Accession No.   1122   Index No. 031/bdch

Title   Sze Shu Kai T<del>iao</del> Ts'o

四 書 改 錯

Classification   A - 131

Subject   Corrections on the Four Books

References

Author   Mao Ch'i Ling of the Ching   清、毛奇齡

Edition   Second edition by Hsueh P'u

Index   Provided

Bound in   1 t'ao, 8 ts'e, mien lien paper

Remarks

The University of Toronto Chinese Library

. . . .

Accession No.   1123   Index No.   042/zmbo

Title   Hsiao Hsüeh Chü Tu Chi
             小 學 句 讀 記

Classification   A - 151

Subject   Dictionaries

References

Author   Wang Chung Fu of the Ching   清 王 仲復

Edition   San Yuen Liu Ch'uan Ching T'an edition

Index   none

Bound in   1 t'ao, 6 chuan, 5 ts'e

Remarks

The University of Toronto Chinese Library

. . . .

Accession No. 1124   Index No.   076/hego

Title   Ch'ing Ting Li Fan Pu Tse Li
         欽 定 理 藩 部 則 例
Classification   B - 62

Subject   Mandates and memorials

References

Author   T'o Chin
          ~~T'uo Ch'ing~~ and others in the Ch'ing period 清, 托津

Edition   34th year of Kwang Hsü, movable type

Index   provided in the second book

Bound in   2 t'ao, 16 t'se, mao pien paper.

Remarks

28

The University of Toronto Chinese Library

. . . .

Accession No.   1125 7   Index No.   067/zcjb

Title   Wen Tzu Meng Ch'iu

文字蒙求

Classification   A - 161

Subject   Graphic dictionaries

References

Author   Lu Yu Yün of the Ching   清·蒙友筠

Edition   30th year of Kwangsu Hsü

Index   None

Bound in   1 t'ao, 4 chuan, 4 tuse

Remarks

The University of Toronto Chinese Library

....

27

Accession No. 1126   Index No. 077/Jcbh

Title   LI Tai Shih Lun

歷代史論

Classification   B - 367

Subject   Expositions on History

References

Author   Chang P'u of the Ming   Edited by   明·張溥;   Commentary & punctuation by   孫執升   Sun Chih-shêng

Edition   Ch'ang Hsun San Fan, Kwang Hsü period

Index   provided

Bound in   2 t'ao, 22 chuan, 12 ts'e

Remarks   white paper

The University of Toronto Chinese Library

....

Accession No.   1127   Index No.   037/zhde

Title   Ta Ch'ing Shih Tsu Chang Huang Ti Sheng Hsün
         大 清 世 祖 章 皇 帝 聖 訓

Classification   B - 67

Subject   Imperial edicts

References

Author   Ch'ing Emperor Jen   清聖祖仁皇帝
          Hand written manuscript
Edition

Index   None

Bound in   1 t'ao 6 chuan, 2 t'se powder paper

Remarks

The University of Toronto Chinese Library

. . . .

Accession No.   1128   Index No. 040/h咢d

Title   Chi Yüan Chi So Chi   寄園寄所寄

Classification   C - 308

Subject   Miscellanous writngs (personal experiences of life)

References

Author   Chao Heng Fu of the Ch'ing 清, 趙恒夫

Edition   Wen Hsiu T'ang

Index   None

Bound in   2 t'ao, 12 chuan, 16 ts'e ¢ powder paper)

Remarks

The University of Toronto Chinese Library

. . . .

/3

Accession No.   1129   Index No.   031/bfoa

Title   Szu Shu T'u Peng   四書讀本

Classification   A - 131

Subject   Readers on the Four Books

References

Author   not stated

Edition   Published during the Ming period

Index   None

Bound in   1 t'ao 5 t'se, Mien Lien paper

Remarks

The University of Toronto Chinese Library

. . . .

Accession No. 1130 ⁴⁹   Index No.   125/zz1

Title   Lao Tze Yi   老子翼

Classification   C - 731

Subject   Taoism

References

Author   Compiled by Chiao Hung of the ~~Ching~~ Ming 焦竑

Edition   published by Ching Hsi Ts'un Hsieh, Kwangsü Hsü 23rd year

Index

Bound in   1 t'ao, 8 chuan, 4 t'se.

Remarks

The University of Toronto Chinese Library

. . . .

Accession No.   1131 [22]   Index No.   128/gdc

Title   Sheng Wu Chi   聖武記

Classification   B -42

Subject   History of the Ch'ing

References

Author   Wei Yüan of the Ch'ing   清魏源

Edition   Ku Wei T'ang

Index   Provided

Bound in   1 t'ao, 14 chuan, 12 ts'e

Remarks

Cab. I

The University of Toronto Chinese Library

....

Accession No.   1132 73   Index No. 030/bmjn

Title   Ku Hsüeh Hui Tsuan   古學彙纂

Classification   c - 13

Subject   Essays on various subjects

References

Author   Chou Shih Yung of the Ming   周時雍

Edition   Ming Ch'ung Cheng

Index   provided

Bound in   1 t'ao, 10 chüan, 16 t'se, bamboo paper

Remarks

The University of Toronto Chinese Library

. . . .

Accession No.   1133 109   Index No.   173/czd

Title   Hsüeh San Chi   雪山集

Classification   D - 53

Subject   A general collection of various subjects

References

Author   Wang Chih of the Sung   宋，王賫

Edition   Pei Yun San Fang
           T'ung Chih period

Index   provided

Bound in   1 t'ao, 6 t'se, Lien shih paper

Remarks

34

The University of Toronto Chinese Library

. . . .

Accession No. 1134 ⁷³   Index No. - 074 - zchi

Title " Yüeh ling tsui pien"
月 令 粹 編

Classification β-157 時令

Subject -(Wylie)- " ..... is a compilation of historical memoranda
for every day in the year ......"

References - Wylie's Notes page 43   Gest No. 153, Toronto Nos. 504, 593

Author - by Chin Chia-mo 秦嘉謨

Edition

Index a general table of contents for 卷首 and 24 chüan

Bound in 1 táo 8 ts'ê

Remarks

The University of Toronto Chinese Library

....

Accession No.   1135   Index No. 053-니ec
                    31

Title   K'angHsi Cheng Yao   康熙政要

Classification   B - 42

Subject   Records of K'angHsi reign

References

Author   Chang Shen Kung of the Ch'ing   清、章梫恭

Edition   Type blocks

Index   provided

Bound in   1 t'ao, 24 chüan, 12 t'se, "YuKwang Yang" paper

Remarks

The University of Toronto Chinese Library

. . . .

Accession No. 1136   112   Index No. 085/lfdz

Title   Ch'ien Hsü ~~Hsan~~ *Hsien* Sheng Wen Chi   潛虛先生文集

Classification   D - 43

Subject   Collection of prose

References

Author   Written by Tai Chien Hsü of the Ch'ing   清、戴潛虛

Edition   K'ang Hsi period

Index   rpovided

Bound in   1 t'ao, 14 chúan, 8 t'se

Remarks

The University of Toronto Chinese Library

. . . .

Accession No. 1137 *120*

Index No. 009/hzib

Title Wei Wen Tuang Kung Yi Shu 倭文端公遺書

Classification D - 43

Subject A collection of prose memorials and petitions

References

Author *Compiled by* Wei Jen of the Ching 倭仁

Edition The 18th year of Kwang *Hsü* su, Mien lien paper

Index none

Bound in 1 t'ao, 10 chüan, 4 t'se.

Remarks

The University of Toronto Chinese Library

. . . .

Accession No.   1138   ⁷²   Index No. *130-2717*

Title   T'ai Ch'ang Hsin Shu   胎產新書

Classification   C - 63

Subject   On pregnancy and birth

References

Author   Wu Yü of the Ch'ing   吳煜

Edition   Kwang Hsü period, Lien Shih paper

Index   provided

Bound in   1 t'ao, 20 chüan, 6 t'se

Remarks

The University of Toronto Chinese Library

. . . .

Accession No.   1139   80   Index No. 072-dczl

Title   Ming ~~Tsai~~ Chai ~~Shiao~~ Hsiao Shih   明齋小識

Classification   C - 368   小說家

Subject   Miscellanous recrods and narratives

References

Author   諸聯軒 of the Tsing Ching   Compiled by Chu Lien.

Edition   Tao Kwang,   Chia Wu year

Index   provided

Bound in   1 t'ao, 12 chüan, 4 t'sê,   bamboo paper

Remarks

Accession No. *1140*　　　　Index No. *77 - l c c g*

Title 歷代地理志韻編今釋 -

Classification *Li Tai Ji Li Chih Yün Pien Chin Shih*

Subject *b181*

References

Author 清李兆洛輯 *Compiled by Ching, Li Shao Lo*

Edition 家藏版 *Private family edition*

竹紙 *Bamboo paper*

Index

Bound in *10 tse*

Remarks

The University of Toronto Chinese Library

....

Accession No. 1141   Index No. 031/七千千尺

Title 四書典故辨正   Szu Shu Tien Ku Pien Cheng

Classification A

Subject

References

Author 清,周理衷   Ch'ing Li Chung

Edition 森寶堂版   Shun Pao Tang edition blocks.

Index

Bound in 26 Ch'uan   6 Ts'e   Bamboo paper

Remarks

The University of Toronto Chinese Library

. . . .

1140, H4# not found

Accession No. ~~###~~ 1142 ^{22} Index No. 077-lcb7

Title 歷代史案 Li Tai Shih An

Classification   B

Subject

References

Author   清   洪亮吉 Ching. Hung Liang-Chi

Edition   聚奎閣 Published by Chü-Kúeiko edition
'Bamboo paper

Index

Bound in   20 Chúan   6 Ts'e

Remarks

The University of Toronto Chinese Library

....

51

Accession No.   1143   Index No. 030-2788

Title   味餘書室隨筆   Wei yü shu shih sui Pi

Classification   C

Subject

References

Author   清   嘉慶帝 Ching, Chia-Ching Emperor

Edition   殿版 Palace ed.

Blocks, "mien lien" paper

Index

Bound in   2 chüan   4 ts'e

Remarks

The University of Toronto Chinese Library
....

Accession No. *111* 1144   Index No. *195-d331*

Title 魯山木先生文集 *Lu Shan Mu Hsien shêng Wên Chi*

Classification D

Subject *a collection of Lu Shan Mu's essays.*

References

Author 清 魯九皋 *Ching, Lu Chiu-Kao*

Edition *Home Library edition "Mao-Pien" paper, Block 11th year of Tao-Kwang (1831)*

Index

Bound in *Tao 16 Chüan 8 tše*

Remarks

The University of Toronto Chinese Library

....

Accession No. *21* 1145   Index No. 072-dec3

Title 明季北畧 Ming Chi Pei Liao

Classification B52 Miscellaneous historical writing

Subject An account of the Northern Expectation of the later part of the Ming Dynasty.

References

Author Edited by 計六奇 of 清 Chi Liu-Chi ching

Edition Published by individual 半松居士 排字本 Pan Sung Chü Shih "Mao-Pien" paper

Index

Bound in 2 t'ao, 24 Chüan 12 t'se

Remarks

The University of Toronto Chinese Library

. . . .

Accession No.   1146 ²⁸   Index No. 007-338ᵇ

Title   二十一史彈詞注 Êrh-Shih-I Shih Tán Tzŭ Chu

Classification   D-38 別集──詩

Subject — (Gest No. 2962) "a very brief synopsis of Chinese history in verse; the period covered being from the earliest times down to the close of the Yüan Dynasty." This item includes the Ming Dynasty.

References — 012-zafk 6/22 Gest No. 2962. Toronto Nos. 862, 1033

Author   明 楊慎 Ming, Yang Shên

Edition   Blocks.
(乾隆 51ᵗʰ yr. of Chien Lung)
white paper

Index   Dated — Chien-Lung "Ping-Wu" 51/1786

Bound in   1 T'ao   11 Chüan   8 tsê

Remarks

The University of Toronto Chinese Library

. . . .

Accession No. 1148 ⁶   Index No. 031-b73ï

Title 四書考輯要 Ssu Shu Kao Chi Yao

Classification A

Subject

References

Author 清陳宏謀 Ching, Chên Hung-Mou

Edition ~~Private Library~~ 培遠堂 Pei-Yüan-Tang blocks.

36ᵗʰ Chiên Kung "mao-Pien" paper

家藏版 — Private family edition

Dated ~~I~~ Chien Kung "Hsin-Hao" 36/1791

Index

Bound in 20 Chüan 10 tsé

Remarks

The University of Toronto Chinese Library

. . . .

102

Accession No.　1149　　　　Index No. 096-33 和

Title　王茗堂集　Yü Ming Tang Chi

Classification　D

Subject

References

Author　明　湯顕祖　Ming, Tang Hsien-Tsu

Edition　Ming blocks.
"Mao-Pien" paper

Index

Bound in　1 t'ao　4 Collections totaling 30 chuan
9 Tsé

Remarks

52

The University of Toronto Chinese Library

. . . .

Accession No. 1150   39   Index No. 146-32b2

Title   西周史徵   *Hsi Chou Shih Cheng*

Classification   B32   Complete historical narratives

Subject   A history on the Western Chou Dynasty.

References

Author   李泰芬   *Li Tai-Fên*

Edition   Private Library Version
16th year of the Republic (1927) metal movable type

Index '

Bound in   1 táo   57 Chüan   6 tz'e

Remarks

The University of Toronto Chinese Library

. . . .

Accession No. *116* *1151*   Index No. *149-χιdd*

Title 諸葛忠武侯全集 *Chu Ko Chung Wu Hou Chüan Chi*

Classification   D

Subject *a collection of complete work by*
诸葛亮
Chu Ko-Liang

References

Author 诸葛亮   *Edited by* 胡升猷 *Hu Shêng-Yu*
Chu-Ko Liang   *of Han*   *of Ching Dynasty*

Edition 光緒戊子年 *Published by* 歧山縣署
"mao-pien" paper   *Chi-Shan Local government*

Index *Dated — Kuang-Hsü "Wu-Tzu" 14//1888*

Bound in *2 Tao, 21 Chüan 12 tze.*

Remarks

54

The University of Toronto Chinese Library

. . . .

Accession No. 1153⁹   Index No. 042-23c3

Title   尚書因文 shang shu yin Wen

Classification   A

Subject

References

Author 清武士·   Compiled by the Ching Dynasty
                                              scholars.
Edition
blocks, bamboo paper.

Index

Bound in   1 táo   6 chüan   4 tśe

Remarks

The University of Toronto Chinese Library

. . . .

Accession No.   1154 ^31   Index No. 030-2213

Title   周季編略   Chou Chi Pien Liao

Classification   B 32   Complete historical narrative

Subject   A chronological narrative of the
~~later~~ Kings of Later Chou dynasty

References

Author   清黄式三   Ching, Huang Shih-San

Edition   Published by Chekiang Bk. Co.
(12ᵗʰ yr of Tung Chih)
Dated — Tung-Chih "Kuei-Yu" 12/1893

Index   none

Bound in   1 tào, four tsê

Remarks

The University of Toronto Chinese Library

. . . .

Accession No. *1155*²   Index No. *109· c d m i*

Title 直省釋奠禮樂記 *Chih sheng Shih* ~~Tsun~~ *Tien Li Yüeh Chi*

Classification   *A*

Subject

References

Author   *not stated*

Edition *(17ᵗʰ year of Kwang Hsü) blocks. "Mien-hien" paper Published by Fu-wen-Chia, Canton.*
         Dated — Kwang-Hsü "Hsin-Mao" 17/1891

Index

Bound in

Remarks   *6 chüan 4 tsè*

The University of Toronto Chinese Library

. . . .

Accession No. 1156⁷   Index No. 120-97 dc

Title 經韻集字析解 Ching Yün Chi Tzu Hsi Chieh

Classification A

Subject

References

Author 熊宇謙   & Ching, Hsü Hsiung Shou-Chien

Edition 道光壬午年 Block. "Mien-lien" paper.

Tientsin
Dated — Too-Kuong "Jèn-Wu" 2/1822

Index

Bound in   2 tse

Remarks

✓

Ↄ Cab. I

The University of Toronto Chinese Library

....

Accession No. 1157 *109*   Index No. 030-b3eg

Title   古文真寶 *Ku Wan Chên Pao*

Classification   D 63

Subject   a collection of classical essays

References

Author   - not stated

Edition   明萬曆十年 White "mien" paper
Dated — Ming, Wan-Li "Kuei-Wei" 11/ 1583

Index

Bound in   20 t'se

Remarks

The University of Toronto Chinese Library

. . . .

Accession No. 1158 ^10   Index No. 031-6717

Title 四書提耳   Ssu Shu Ti' Erh

Classification   A

Subject

References

Author 清 耿垓   Ching, Kêng Tsai

Edition 1st of Chien Lung
"Lien-Shih" paper. block

Index Dated — Chien-Lung "Ping-Chên" 1/1736

Bound in   1

Remarks

60

The University of Toronto Chinese Library

. . . .

Accession No. *1159* ²⁵   Index No. *149.06 kb*

Title   讀史鏡古編 *Tu Shih Ching Ku Pien*

Classification   *B*

Subject

References

Author   清. 潘世恩 *Ching, Pan Shih-En*

Edition   冶城飛霞閣重刻 *Yeh-Ch'eng, Fei-Hsia-Ko*
毛邊紙 *"Mao-Pien" paper*

Index

Bound in

Remarks   *32 Chüan   8 tsê*

The University of Toronto Chinese Library
....

Accession No. 1160 ^{23} Index No. 162-gnio

Title 通鑑輯覽 Tung Chien Chi Lan

Classification B

Subject

References

Author 清乾隆帝 commentary by the Emperor Chien Lung

Edition Official Version by Emperor Chien-Lung
Bamboo paper

Index

Bound in 8 Táo 120 Chüán 60 Tse

Remarks

The University of Toronto Chinese Library

. . . .

Accession No. *1161* ⁹⁹   Index No. *030-bql*

Title 古詩選 *Ku Shih Hsüan*

Classification   *D*

Subject

References

清 王士禛

Author   *Edited by Wang Shih-Chen of Ching*

Edition 同治五年刻本 毛边纸 *"Mao-Pien" paper*
Dated — Tung-Chih "Ping-Ying" 5/1866

Index

Bound in   *1 Chüan   12 Tsé*

Remarks

The University of Toronto Chinese Library

. . . .

Accession No. 1162 ⁹⁸   Index No. 018-mgie

Title 劉誠意伯文集 Liu Chéng I Po Wên Chi

Classification D

Subject Collection of Liu Chi's essays

References

Author Liu Chi of Ming Dynasty 劉基

Edition 南田果育堂藏版 Nan-Tien-Ko-Yü-Tang edition block Preserved private printed
粉紙夾板 "Fen" paper block wooden-folder

Index

Bound in 1 ~~Chüan~~ Tāo 20 Chüan 7 tsé

Remarks

The University of Toronto Chinese Library

....

Accession No. 1163 62

Index No. 149-gehk

Title 說岳全傳 Shuo Yüeh Chüan Chüan

Classification C

Subject a life story of famous Sung General Yoa (岳) Fei
(yüeh)

References

Author 清 錢 彩 編次 edited in both order by Ching, Chien Tsai

Edition 大文堂版 毛邊紙 Ta-Wei-Tang blocks "Mao-Pien" paper

Index

Bound in 1 t'ao 20 chüan 10 ts'e

Remarks

The University of Toronto Chinese Library

. . . .

Accession No. 1164 39   Index No. 169. *k9k*

Title 關帝事蹟徵信編 *Kuan Ti Shih Chi Cheng Hsin Pien*

Classification B

Subject *Some comments on the life story of Kwang Yü Kuan*

References

Author 清 周廣業 崔應榴 *Ch'ing, Chou Kuang-Yeh and Tsui Ying-ts'ao*

Edition 京都甕城關帝廟藏版 光緒八年刻 錦連紙 夾版 *Ching-Tu. Weng Cheng Kuan-Ti-Miao edition blocks preserved "Tien-Lien" paper. Book Dated — Kuang-Hsü "Jen-Wu" 8/1882 Wooden-folder*

Index

Bound in 1 t'ao 30 Chüan + 1 supplement

Remarks

The University of Toronto Chinese Library

....

Accession No. 1165²⁷   Index No. 140-jbid

Title   蒙古遊牧記 Mang Ku Yu Ma Chi

Classification B 222

Subject   An account of Nomadic Life
travelling through Mongolia

References

Author   清 張穆 撰, ʷʳⁱᵗᵗᵉⁿ ᵇʸ ching. Chang Mu

Edition 壽陽祁氏刊 同治六年刻 Shou-Yang-Chi-Shih published at
Bamboo paper
Dated — Tung-Chih "Ting-Mao" 6/1867

Index

Bound in 1 t'ao   16 chüan   8 ts'e

Remarks

The University of Toronto Chinese Library

. . . .

Accession No. 1166¹¹⁹   Index No. 030-bji

Title   古謠諺 Ku ~~~~ Yao Yen

Classification   D

Subject   a collection of ancient proverbs
+ old sayings

References

Author   Edited by 杜文瀾 of Ch'ing
                    Tu Wên Lan

Edition   曼陀羅華閣精刊本 Man-To-Lo-Hua-Ko Fine-printed.
          咸豐辛酉年刊

                              Bamboo paper
Index   Dated — Hsien-Fêng "Hsin-yu" 11/1861

Bound in

Remarks   2 Táo   100 Chüan 16 tsé

The University of Toronto Chinese Library

....

Accession No. *1167*[19]   Index No. *169- 大3 9 夫*

Title 關帝聖蹟圖志 *Kuang Ti sheng chi Tu chih*

Classification β

Subject *a pictorial life story y kwang yü.*
pictorial

References 清 盧湛 *Ching, Lu Chan*

Author

Edition 于成龍鑒定本 *Yü Chêng-Lung edition*
毛邊紙 *"Mao-Pien" paper*

Index

Bound in   1 *t'ao*   5 *chüan*   5 *tsê*

Remarks

The University of Toronto Chinese Library
....

Accession No. 1168 98   Index No. 030-bzlj

Title 古文辭類纂 Ku Wen Tzu Lei Tsuan

Classification D

Subject

References 清姚鼐撰

Author Written by Ching, Yao Nai

Edition 問竹軒新刻本 Wên-Chu-Hsüan block printed edition.
同治八年刻 dated Tung-Chih 8/1869
mien hien paper

Index

Bound in   1 tao   75 chüan   16 tsê

Remarks

The University of Toronto Chinese Library

· ·

Accession No.   1169   *116*   Index No. 067-3343

Title   文心雕龍輯註 Wên Hsin Tiao Lung chi Chu

Classification   D

Subject

References

Author   Compiled by 劉勰 Liu Hsieh
Notes by 黄敬崑 Huang Ching-Kun

Edition   太史連紙 貴文堂藏版   *blocks preserved*
"Tai-Shih-Lien" paper   Kuei-Wên-Tang edition

Index

Bound in   1 Tao, 10 Chüan, 4 Tse

Remarks

The University of Toronto Chinese Library

. . . .

Accession No. 1170 ² Index No. 031-68cj

Title 四書合講 Ssŭ Shu Ho Chiang

Classification A

Subject

References

Author 清 翁復 ~~Edited~~ Chíng, Weng Fu

Edition 愛日堂刻本 毛太紙
Ai-jih-Táng block printed, "mao-tai" paper edition

Index

Bound in 2 tǎo 12 ts̆e

Remarks

The University of Toronto Chinese Library
....

Accession No. 1171⁵   Index No. 012-bjcc

Title 公穀合刊 Kung Ku Ho Kan

Classification A

Subject

References

Author (Edited by 王崑繩) Ching)
        Ching, Wang Kun-Shêng
Edition 仿宋刻本 mien hien paper
         Imitation of Sung Block print

Index

Bound in 1 t'ao   6 tsê

Remarks

The University of Toronto Chinese Library
. . . .

Accession No. 1172²⁶   Index No. 166-dné

Title 野獲編 Yeh Hüo Pien

Classification B

Subject

References

Author 清 沈德符 Chíng, Shên Tê-Fu

Edition 扶荔山房刊 Fu-Li-Shan-Fang edition block-engraving
道光年刻. 竹紙 dated Tao-Kuang period (1821-1850)
Bamboo paper

Index

Bound in 2 Táo 30 Chüan 20 Tśe

Remarks

The University of Toronto Chinese Library
. . . .

Accession No. ⁵⁵ 1173   Index No. 009-nmmg

Title 儒學警悟 Ju Hsüeh Ching Yü Wu

Classification C

Subject

References

Author Edited by 清 俞鼎孫 俞経 Ching, Yü Ting-Sun and Yü Ching

Edition 文楷齋刻版 Wên-Kai-Chai printed edition engraved blocks.
單宣紙 "Tan-Hsüan" paper

Index 1 tao. 7 chüan (7集) 10 ts'e
                              7 chi
Bound in

Remarks

72

The University of Toronto Chinese Library

....

Accession No. 1174[46] Index No. 170 - h3c3

Title 陳氏中西回史日曆 Ch'ên Shih Chung Hsi ~~Hui~~ Hui Shih Jih Li

Classification B-157

Subject a comparative calendar of Chinese & Mohamedan years.

References

Author Ch'ên Yüan 陳垣

Edition National Peking University Chinese Classic Series
Metal moval types with red & black colours.

Index 粉連紙
"Fên-lien" paper

Bound in 1 T'ao 20 Chüan 5 Ts'e

Remarks

The University of Toronto Chinese Library
....

Accession No.   1176¹¹⁰   Index No. 085-jid

Title   滑疑集   Hua I Chi

Classification   D

Subject

References

Author   韓,錫胙 Han Hsi-Tso of Ch'ing Dynasty

Edition   同治年刻 連史紙 dated Tung-Chih period (1862-1874)
浙江處州府署藏板 Chih-Chiang Chu-Chou Fu-Shu edition block Preserved
"Lien-Shih" paper

Index

Bound in   1 t'ao   8 ch'üan   4 ts'e

Remarks

The University of Toronto Chinese Library

. . . .

Accession No. 1177 60 Index No. 149.03ᶜ

Title 讀書說記 *Tu Shu Chi* *shuo*

Classification C

Subject

References

Author 清 胡承諾 *Ching, Hu Chêng-No*

Edition 三餘草堂版 *San-Yü-Tang Sao-Tang edition woodblocks*
光緒年刻 *dated Kuang-Hsü period (1875-1908)*
毛邊紙 *"Mao-Pien" paper*

Index

Bound in 1 tao 4 chüan 6 tse with

Remarks chronology

78

The University of Toronto Chinese Library

. . . .

Accession No. 1178¹¹¹   Index No. 140-93 b k

Title 蘇長公家語 *Su Cháng Kung Mi Yü*

Classification D

Subject

References

Author ~~Edited by~~ 明 吳京 *Ming, Wu ching*

Edition 明天啓年刻版 硃批評點 精刻本 *block-Engraved*
明錦紙 *dated Ming, Tien-Chi period (1621-1627)*
commentaries printed in red. fine printed edition
"*Ming-mien*" *paper*

Index

Bound in 2 *Tao* 16 *Chüen* 10 *Tsé*

Remarks

Cab I

77

Accession No.   1179 92   Index No. 140-0331

Title 藝文珠璣類編 I Wên Chu Chi Lei Pien

Classification D

Subject

References

Author Edited & Compiled by 章伯棠
                              Chang Po-Tang

Edition 抄本   白棉紙
manuscript , "Pai-Mien" paper

Index

Bound in   2 T'ao   16 Tsê

Remarks

80

The University of Toronto Chinese Library

....

Accession No.   1180   Index No. 011-38hh

Title   兩晉清談 Liang Chin Ching Tan

Classification   C 328   Extracts from various
                           works compiled & edited.

Subject

A collection of terms, phraseologies &
stories of the 2 TSIN dynasties.

References

Author   清 沈杲之 Ching, Shên Kao-chih

Edition   嘉慶庚申年鐫 "mien-lien" pages

          王如金校刊, 盡簪堂藏版 巾箱本精刻   (printed)

          Wang Ju-Chin revised, Ho-Tsan-Tang edition, pocket edition, fine)
                                 block preserved

Index

Bound in   1 t'ao   12 chüan   6 ts'e

Remarks

The University of Toronto Chinese Library

. . . .

Accession No.   1181   50

Index No. 146-zic

Title   西廂記   Hsi Hsiang Chi

Classification   C - 387

Subject   The Romance of the West Chamber.
— a love story

References

Author   not stated

Edition   此宜閣博訂本   Tzü I Ko edition
綿連紙硃批
"mienlien" paper, commentaries printed in red

Index

Bound in   1 tʻao   6 tsʻe

Remarks

The University of Toronto Chinese Library

. . . .

Accession No.   1182 ^10   Index No. 149-
037- 3m
002-c h
009- え l

Title   大學 論語, 中庸 傳註 *Ta Hsüeh, Lun Yü, Chung Yung, Chuan Chu*

Classification   A-131

Subject   a commentary studies on the Classics.

References

Author   明. 李塨 *Ming, Li Kung*

Edition   Metal printed. "Mien-Lien" paper

Index

Bound in   1 Tao,   4 Tse

Remarks

The University of Toronto Chinese Library

. . . .

63 or 8

Accession No.   1183   Index No. 037-33 lj

Title   Yuan Chuen Chiu

大方廣,圓覺修多羅了義經   Ta Fang Kuan Yüan chüeh Hsiu
                              To Lo Liao I ching

Classification   C - 513   Buddhism

Subject   a Tang Dynasty Translation of the
           Buddhist Bible

References

釋佛陀多羅

Author   Translated by Buddhist monk Fro Lo

Edition   Block. 夾連紙.
           "Chia-lien" paper

Index   none

Bound in   1 tăo   2 tsĕ

Remarks

The University of Toronto Chinese Library

. . . .

Accession No. 1184   Index No. 075-kml

Title 樗繭譜 chien Pu   Agriculture

Classification C 539   Miscellaneous scientific work

Subject A book on silk industry with
an account of raising silk
worms in Chuan Yi.

References

Author 清鄭珍纂 莫友芝註   Compiled by Ching, Chêng Chên (纂)
Annotated by Mo Yu-Chih (註)

Edition 獨山莫氏刊本 道光十七年刻 貴州綿紙
Tu-Shan, Mo-Shih edition, dated Tao-Kuang 17/1837. 10th year of Tao Kuang( ) "Kuei-Chou Mien paper"

Index

Bound in 1 t'ao 2 ts'e

Remarks

The University of Toronto Chinese Library

. . . .

Accession No. 1185   Index No. 070-3391

Title 方言疏證 Fang Yen Su Chêng

Classification A 156 訓詁 Analogic dictionaries

Subject A dictionary on the words y different dialects

References

Author 清戴震著 Ching, Tai Chen

Edition 漢青篋刊微波榭本 Han Ching-I printed, Wei-Po-Hsieh edition
光緒年刊 綿連紙 dated Kuang-Hsü period (1875-1908)
"Mien-Lien" paper

Index

Bound in — Tao 13 Chüan 4 Tse.

Remarks

✓
Cab. I

40

The University of Toronto Chinese Library
....

40

Accession No. 1186   Index No. 146-ykjh

Title 西域瑣談 Hsi yü So Tán

Classification B 196

Subject

References

Author 椿園七十一著 Chün Yüan Chi-Shih-I

Edition 抄寫本   Bamboo paper
         Manuscript

Index

Bound in 1 tao 4 tse.

Remarks

70

The University of Toronto Chinese Library
. . . .

Accession No. *1187* 70 Index No. *030-gju*

Title 唐語林 *Tǎng yǔ Lin*

Classification *C*

Subject

References

Author 宋 王讜撰 *Selected by Wang Tang g the Sung Dynasty*

Edition 湖北官書處刊 守山閣本 *Hu-Pei, Kuan shu-chü edition*
光緒年刻 白綿紙 *dated Kuang Hsü period (1875-1908) White mien paper*

Index

Bound in *1 Tǎo*   *8 chüan*   *4 tse*

Remarks

88

pl ✓ ✗   ✓   86
                                                        ✓   Cab I

The University of Toronto Chinese Library

. . . .

✓ Accession No. 1188 ⁸⁴   Index No. 118-ggmg

Title 竹窗遺筆 Chu Chuang Sui Pi

Classification C-513

Subject

References

Author 明 釋袾宏著 Ming, Shih Chu-Hung

Edition 明萬曆版精刻本   白紙
Ming Wan Li period (1573-1619)   White paper
fine printed edition

Index

Bound in   1 tʻao   6 tsʻe

Remarks

The University of Toronto Chinese Library
....

Accession No. 1189 ⁶⁰   Index No. 052-ie ha

Title 幾何原本 Chi Ho Yüan Pên.

Classification   C

Subject a book on Geometry
Translated by Ricci
Matteo

References

Author 利瑪竇译   徐光啟筆受
Li Ma-Tou translated, Hsü Kuang-Chi (筆受)

Edition Home Library
同治四年刊)   Bamboo paper
4 th year of Tung chih (   )
dated Tung-chih 4/1865

Index

Bound in 2 táo   8 tsê.

Remarks

√illus.
√

88
√

The University of Toronto Chinese Library
. . . .

Accession No. _1190⁷_   Index No. _031-67kz_

Title   四書圖考 Ssŭ Shu Tu Kao

Classification   A

Subject

References

Author   清 杜炳學   Ching, Tu Ping-hsüeh ~~Tu~~ ~~hsüeh~~

Edition   ~~Home Library~~ "Mien-Liao" paper
家藏版 Private family edition

Index

Bound in   2 t'ao.   12 ts'e.

Remarks

The University of Toronto Chinese Library

. . . .

Accession No. *1191"*   Index No. *089-jdɛ̌z*

Title 爾雅直音   *Êrh   ya chih Yin*

Classification A ~~161~~ 156 字書. *Graphic dictionaries*

Subject *a historical study of some terms & words in Er ya.*

References

Author *Edited by* 孫佲 (*Sun Pin*) *of the Ching Dynasty*

Edition 天心閣藏版 嘉慶 巳未 增訂本
*Tien-Hsin-ko edition dated Chia-Ching "Soŭ-Wei"/1799
bamboo paper   Chi*

Index *none*

Bound in *1 tao.   2 chüan = 2 ts'e*

Remarks

The University of Toronto Chinese Library

. . . .

Accession No. *1192* ^28^   Index No. *032-leae*

Title 增註千姓聯珠 *Tsêng chu chien Hsing Lien Chu*

Classification B 337 ?

Subject *a comprehensive study on different origins of Chinese surnames*

References

Author 清潘綃佩著 楊宗楷 增註
        Ching, Pán gên-Pei (著), Yang Tsung-Kai (增註) Amended Annotations

Edition *Home Library*
        道光七年刻 綿連紙
        7th year of Tao Kuang) "Mien-Lien" paper

Index *dated Tao-Kuang ⑦/1837   "Mien-Lien" paper*

Bound in   *1 t'ao   4 chüan = 4 t'sê*

Remarks

The University of Toronto Chinese Library

....

Accession No. 1193   Index No. 007-bdej

Title 井眉居雜著 *Ching Mei Chü Tsa Chu*

Classification C 308   Miscellaneous writings

Subject a collection of essays on various topics

References

Author Edited by 姚前機 *Yao Chien-Chi*

Edition Home Library White paper
家藏版 *Private family edition*

Index

Bound in 1 Tao 1 Tse.

Remarks

The University of Toronto Chinese Library

. . . .

Accession No. 1194   70   Index No. 124-eee

Title 習是編 Hsi shih Pien

Classification C 328   Extracts from various works

Subject Compiled works on daily life

References

Author 汪聚鑰 of the Ching Dynasty
Wang Chü-yao

Edition Home Library 乾隆年刻 三餘堂藏 毛邊紙
家藏版 Private family edition dated Chien-lung period, San Yü Tang edition, "mao-pien" paper
(1736-1795)

Index

Bound in 1 t'ao 2 ts'e.

Remarks

√√
~'9

The University of Toronto Chinese Library
....

√ <u>Accession No.</u> 1195 '19   <u>Index No.</u> 030-68

<u>Title</u> 史畧   Shih Lüeh

<u>Classification</u> B-367.

<u>Subject</u>

<u>References</u>

<u>Author</u> 宋 高似孫輯 Compiled by Sung, Kao Ssŭ-Sun

<u>Edition</u> 仿宋. 宋一麈木刻 Imitation of Sung edition block engraving
洋粉連紙 Sung I-chên printed
imported Western "Fên-lien" paper

<u>Index</u>

<u>Bound in</u> 1 t'ao, 6 chüan   2 ts'e

<u>Remarks</u>

107 ✓

The University of Toronto Chinese Library

. . . .

107

Accession No. 1196   Index No. 085-ljbd

Title 潛園友朋書問 chien yüan yu p'êng shu wên

Classification D43 Prose

Subject a collection of handwriting correspondences of some distinguished literati of the Ching Dynasty.

References

Author Edited by 存齋 Tsun-Chai

Edition Home Library. Blocks made from the original writings. "Lien-shih" paper

Index 家藏版 Private family edition

Bound in 1 t'ao   12 chüan   2 ts'ê

Remarks

100

The University of Toronto Chinese Library

. . . .

Accession No. 1197 ^100^   Index No. 075-gc gr

Title 梅村家藏稿   *Mei Tsun Chia Tsang Kao*

Classification D 208

Subject

References

Author 吳偉業 *of the Ching dynasty*
Ching, Wu Wei-Yeh

Edition 董氏誦芬室刊 *Tsung-Shih Sung-Fên-Shih edition*   *block engraving*

宣統三年刻 *"Mien-Lien" paper*

Index *dated Hsüan-Tung 3/1911*

Bound in 1 tao   58 Chüan   8 tsê.

Remarks

98

The University of Toronto Chinese Library

....

Accession No. 1198 ^107^   Index No. 009-ezeb

Title 何文定公集 Ho Wên Ting Kung Chi

Classification D

Subject

References

Author 明, 柏齋先生著 Ming, Po-Chai Hsien Shêng

Edition 明萬曆四年重刊   明白綿紙

dated Ming. Wan-Li 4/1576 reprinted edition "Ming-Pai-Mien" paper

Index 1 t'ao   11 Chüan   4 tsé

Bound in

Remarks

106

The University of Toronto Chinese Library

. . . .

Accession No. 1199 [106]   Index No. 030-97aa

Title 唐詩三百首註疏 Táng Shih San Pai Shou Chu Su

Classification D 68

Subject a commentary study on the 300 Tang poems

References

Author 清蘅塘退士手編, 章燮註
edited by Ching, Hêng-Táng-Túi-Shih (手編), Chang Hsieh (註) Annotations

Edition 宋氏巷兩樓印 白竹紙
Sung-Shih Chüan-Yü-Lou printed, white bamboo paper

Index

Bound in   1 chüan   6 tsé.

Remarks

The University of Toronto Chinese Library

. . . .

Accession No. *1200*[85]   Index No. 061-imie

Title 感應篇註釋全解 *Kan Ying Pien Chu Shih Chüan Chieh*

Classification C

Subject

References

Author *unknown.*

Edition 乾隆年刻 竹紙
dated Chien-lung period (1736-1795) , Bamboo paper

Index

Bound in

Remarks

. . . .

Accession No. *50* *1201*   Index No. *113/mfge*

Title 禮書通故 *Li Shu Tung Ku*

Classification *A61*

Subject

References

Author 黃以周 字元同 *1828-1899 Huang I Chou*

Edition 黃氏試館刊本 1893 (光緒十九年)
      Huang Shih shih Kuan block-print edition

Index

Bound in *4 táo 38 tśe*

Remarks

102

2

The University of Toronto Chinese Library

· ·

Accession No.　1202　　　　Index No. 106- aa ṭP#

Title　百尺樓叢畫　Pai Chih Lou Tsung Hua

Classification　C-223　Calligraphy & Painting

Subject　Coloured pictures

References

Author　清. 王耀如. Ch'ing, Wang Yao-ju.　Wang Yao-ju

Edition　石印著色　錦連紙　Shih Yin Chu Sü, mien
"mien-lien" paper　Lien Chi.
Lithographic edition (colored)

Index

Bound in　1 t'ao　8 chuan　8 ts'e

Remarks

103

The University of Toronto Chinese Library

. . . .

Accession No. *1203*   Index No. 077-ǰccʠ

Title 歷代名臣言行錄   Li Tai Ming Chen Yen Hsing Lu

Classification B717

Subject

References

Author 清 朱桓轄   Compiled by Ching, Chu Huan

Edition 蔚齋藏版 Wei-chai (Tsáng Pan) edition

素慶丁巳新鎸 綿連紙 夾版   Chia'Ching "Ting-Ssŭ" / 1797 Chia Ching Ting Ssŭ Hsin chün

Index   1797   "Mienpaa Lien" chih paper   Chia Pan wood block

Bound in   1 táo, 24 chüan   32 tsè

Remarks

104

The University of Toronto Chinese Library

. . . .

Accession No.   1204   Index No.   154-Lccbfinta

Title   賞奇軒四種合編 Shang Chi *hsüan* Ssŭ Chung Ho Pien

Classification   C 223 Calligraphy & Painting

Subject   A collection of 4 books dealing with
          the painting of portraits, bamboo, the way
          the same of chessing & calligraphy with illustrations

References

Author   Unknown

Edition   文德堂版 Wên-Tê-Tang ~~Pao~~ edition blocks.
          連史纸本 "Lien-Shih" *paper* ~~cloth~~

Index   none

Bound in   1 Tao   4 tse.

Remarks

131

The University of Toronto Chinese Library

....

Accession No. *1205*　　　　　　　　　Index No. *120- ld ku hi*

Title　　*續集 漢印分韻* *Hsü Chi* *Han Yin Fêw Yün*

Classification　　*C 223 seals + seal cutting*

Subject　　or *雜部 Tsa Pu. Miscel-*

References

Author　　*Edited by* *Hsieh Ching-Yang* *謝景仰 g the Chíng Dynasty*

Edition　　*漱藝室藏版 Su-Yin-Tang (Tsang Pan) block preserved edition*
嘉慶八年出版 連史紙 Chia-Ching Pa Nien Chu Pan
癸亥 8/1803 "Kuei-Hai" 8/1803
"Lien Shih" paper

Index

Bound in　　*1 tao　　2 chuan　　2 tsê*

Remarks

106

The University of Toronto Chinese Library

. . . .

Accession No. 1206   Index No. 147-R h h h gkd

Title 觀無量壽佛經圖頌 Kuan Wu Liang Shou Fo Ching Tu
                                         Sung.

Classification   C 513   Buddhism

Subject

References

Author   Edited by Chang Wên Chia 張文嘉 of the Ching Dynasty.

Edition   Home Library. 順治年刊 Shun-Chih Hsien Hô
                                                   period (1653-1661)
          Bamboo paper
          竹紙 Chu Chih   Bamboo paper

Index

Bound in   1 tao   4 tsé

Remarks

The University of Toronto Chinese Library

. . . .

Accession No. *1207*   Index No. 001- dgigb

Title   世說新語補 *Shih Shuo Hsin Yü Pu*

Classification C 368

Subject

References

Author 宋劉義慶撰, 梁劉孝標註 *Written by Sung, Liu Yü-Ching. Liang, Liu St Hsiao Piao Dynasty (Annotated)*

Edition 明刻本 書林余地儒梓 *Ming Ko Pen (1368-1652) Shu Lin Yü-I Ju Tsü*
竹紙夾板 *Chu Chih Chia Pen Bamboo paper Wood Block*

Index

Bound in 1 Tao   20 Chuan   6 Tse

Remarks

The University of Toronto Chinese Library

· ·

Accession No. 1208   Index No. 030·bbee

Title 古今秘苑 Kŭ Chin Pii yüan

Classification C-328

Subject

References

Author 十二桐樓主人 Shih Êrh Túng Lou Chu Jên

Edition 原刻本, 袖珍本 Yüan Kô Pên Haiu Chên Pên
        Original Block-printing edition,
        Pocket edition
        竹紙 Chu Chih Bamboo paper

Index

Bound in 1 t'ao, 32 chuan 6 t'se.

Remarks

The University of Toronto Chinese Library

. . . .

Accession No. 1210   Index No. 033-iece

Title   書是紀始 I shih chi shih

Classification   C 303

Subject   A book of Origin & other ritual practice

References

Author   清 祝亭著 Ching, Chu Ting

Edition   Home Library
光緒辛卯年刻竹紙 京都文奎堂藏版
Kuang-Shü Hsin-Mao Nien Kô Chu Chih Ching-Tu, Wên-Kuei-Tang ed.
Hsii Hsin-Mao° Bamboo paper.   Tsang Pan
Index   #1891   17/1891   block preserved

Bound in   1 táo   22 Chuan   6 t'se.

Remarks

110

12

The University of Toronto Chinese Library

. . . .

Accession No.   1212   Index No. 072·嶼太14

Title   昆青堂詩集 Yü Ching Táng Shih Chi

Classification   D 38 Verse

Subject

References

Author   吳脈卷著 Wu Mai Ch'ang

Edition Private Editions 吳佩孚刊 王芝祥訂
(民國十一年刻) 連史紙 硃印 Printed in red
Wu P'ei-Fu (Kan) & Wang Chih-Hsiang (Ting) Min Kuo Shih I Nien K'o
"Lien-Shih" Chih Chu Yin
          paper

Index   Dated, 1922 (Ming-Kuo 11 Nien)

Bound in   1 tao   4 Chuan   4 t'se.

Remarks

The University of Toronto Chinese Library

....

Accession No. *1213* Index No. *072-edgg*

Title 春秋穀梁傳註 *Ch'un Chiu Ku Liang Chuan Chu*

Classification **A** *101*

Subject

References

Author 柯劭忞 *K'o Shao Min*

Edition 鉛印本 洋毛邊紙 *Hsüeh Yin Pen "Yang-Mao-Pien" Chih paper Type-setting edition*

Index *none* 1 *t'ao* 14 *chüan* 4 *ts'e*

Bound in

Remarks

The University of Toronto Chinese Library

· ·

Accession No. *1214*   Index No. *009- n⅗eg*

Title 儒門法語 *Ju Mên Fa Yü*

Classification   *C*

Subject

References

Author 清彭建求編 *edited by* *Ching, Pêng Ting-Chiu Bien*

Edition *Private block Edition*
乾隆三十五年刊 竹紙
Chien-Lung San Shih Wu Nien Kan   Bamboo paper

Index *Dated, Chien-Lung "Kêng-Ying" 35/1770*

Bound in   *1 tao   2 tsê*

Remarks

73

The University of Toronto Chinese Library

. . . .

Accession No. *1215*   Index No. 039-m989

Title 學海津梁 Hsüeh Hai Chin Liang

Classification C 308 Miscellaneous writings, discussion
+ Exposition.

Subject
A collection of essays on Chinese
Educational systems + methods.

References

Author 清, 崔學古編輯, *edited by* Ch'ing. Ts'ui Hsüeh-Ku ~~Pien Chi~~

Edition 文起堂刊 康熙年刊, 毛邊紙
Wên-Chi Tang Kan Kang Hsi Nien Kan "Mao-Pien" chih paper
Dated, Kāng-Hsi period (1660—1722)

Index 1 tao 4 chuan 2 t'se

Bound in

Remarks

114

117

The University of Toronto Chinese Library

....

Accession No. 1216   Index No. 060-ggdb大才

Title 徐文集四聲猿 Hsü Wên Chi Ssŭ Shêng Yüan

Classification D 147 Ballads 小調 Hsiao Tiao

Subject a sacaristical story with colloquial presentation

References

Author 明 徐渭撰   袁宏道評點
Written by Ming, Hsü Wei Chun   Yüan Hung-Tao Ping Tien commentaries
Edition 明刻本, 毛邊係 Ming Dynastie (1368-1643) black printed ed.
Ming K'o Pên, "Mao-Pien" thin paper

Index

Bound in 1 t'ao   1 tsê.

Remarks

115

The University of Toronto Chinese Library

. . . .

Accession No. 1217   Index No. 130-e/e3

Title 胎產秘書 Tái Chǎn Pi Shu

Classification C M 90   Gynecology & Obstetrics

Subject a manual on obstetrics.

References

Author

Edition Home library Edition
绵連紙
"Mien-Lien" cloth paper

Index

Bound in 1 t'ao 3 chüan 2 ts'e.

Remarks

The University of Toronto Chinese Library

· ·

1110

Accession No. *1218*　　　　Index No. *024 - az6g7c*

Title　千文六書統要　*Chien Wên Liu Shu Túng Yao*

Classification　*A 161*　　　*Graphic dictionaries.*

Subject　*a graphic dictionary on characters used in the 6 classes.*

References

Author　明 胡正言 輯篆　*Compiled by Ming, Hu Chêng-Yen Chi Chuan*

Edition　十竹齋藏版. 竹紙　*Shih—Chu—Chai edition Tsang Pan Chu Chih Bamboo paper*

Index　*none*

Bound in　*1 tao　2 chuan　4 tsi.*

Remarks

The University of Toronto Chinese Library

· ·

Accession No. 1279   Index No. 124-ℓmcqᵗᵗ

Title 翻譯名義集選 Fan Yi Ming Yi Chi Hsüan

Classification C 513 Buddhism

Subject An interpretation of the translated Buddhist terms.

References

Author

Edition 精刻本 毛邊紙 ~~Ching K'o Pên~~ "Mao-Pien" ~~Chih~~ paper Fine-printed edition

Index 1 tao 2 chüan 2 tsé

Bound in

Remarks

118

16

The University of Toronto Chinese Library

....

Accession No. 1220   Index No. 085-bgcde

Title 求闕齋弟子記 Chiu Chüeh Chai Ti Tzŭ Chi

Classification

Subject

References

Author 清王定安譔 Ching, Wang Ting-An Chuan

Edition 京都龍文齋藏版 Ching-Tu Lung-Wên-Chai edition Tsang Pan blok preserved
光緒二年刊　綿連紙 Kuang Hsü Erh Nien Kan "Mien-Lien" Chih paper
Index　Dated, Kuang-Hsü "Ping-Tzŭ" 2/1876

Bound in 1 Tʻao 32 Chüan, 16 tsê.

Remarks

Accession No. *1221*   Index No. *030-edgj*

Title 周易達源 *Chou ẜI Fêng Yüan*

Classification *A — 11*

Subject

References

Author 清, 馮光炳著 *Ching. Fêng Kuang-Ping Chu*

Edition 寫本   綿連紙
Hsieh Pên "Mien-lien" Chih paper
maniscript copy

Index

Bound in *1 tao, 10 tśe*

Remarks

21

Cab. I

120

The University of Toronto Chinese Library

· ·

Accession No.   *1222*   Index No. *018-gbdc tcm*

Title   則古昔齋筭學 *Tsê Tsê Ku Hsi Chai Suan Hsüeh*

Classification   *C 138   Mathematics*

Subject

References

Author   清李善蘭 *Ching, Li Shan-Lan*

Edition   家藏版,   同治丁卯年刊 *Private family edition*

Home Library Chia Tsang Pan,   Tung Chih Ting Mao Nien Kan

竹紙

Index   *Chu Chih*   *Dated, Tung-Chih "Ting-Mao" 6/1867*
        Bamboo paper

Bound in   1 *táo*   6 *tsê*

Remarks

121

23

61

The University of Toronto Chinese Library

....

Accession No. *1223*   Index No. *166-bm*

Title   重學 *Chung Hsüeh*

Classification   *C138 Mathmatics*

Subject

References *Translated orally by Ai-Yüeh-Sè (England). Recorded by Li Shan-Lau, Ching Dynasty*

Author 英國艾約瑟口譯,   清李善蘭筆述
Ying Kuo Ai-Yüeh-Sè (England) translated   Ching, Li Shan-Lang Pi Shu written

Edition *Home Library*

同治五年刊, 竹紙.
Túng Chih Wu Nien Kan, Chu Chih Bamboo paper
Dated, Túng-Chih "Ping-Ying" 5/1866

Index

Bound in *1 tao   6 tse.*

Remarks

122

24

The University of Toronto Chinese Library

. . . .

Accession No. *1224*   Index No. *067-ghdb*

Title 文徵明甫田集 *Wên Chêng Ming Fu Tien Chi*

Classification D

Subject

References

Author 明　文徵明撰 *Written by* *Ming, Wên Chêng-Ming* ~~Chuen~~

Edition *Lithographic Version*
宣统三年印 *Hsüan Tung San Nien Yin*
粉纸 *"fên" chih paper*

Index *Dated, Hsüan-Tung "Hsing-Hai" 3/1911*

Bound in *1 tao　36 chuan　6 tsé*

Remarks

The University of Toronto Chinese Library
....

√ √
Cab. I

Accession No. *1225*   Index No. *030-b)n*

Title   古詩歸 *Ku Shih Kuei*

Classification   *D-68*

Subject

References

Author   明 鍾惺譚遠 *Selected by Ming, Chung Hsing and others* ~~Tang Hsüan Tang Ting~~

Edition *Wood block*. 明萬曆丁巳年刻
         竹紙 *Ming Wan Li Ting Ssŭ Nien K'o*
         ~~Chu Chih~~ *Bamboo paper Dated, Ming, Wan-Li "Ting-Ssu" 45/1817*

Index   *1 Tao   12 Chuan   4 Tse.*

Bound in

Remarks

55

The University of Toronto Chinese Library

. . . .

Accession No. 1226   Index No. 178-吴吴

Title 韓子粹言 Han Tʒǔ Sʒui Yen

Classification C

Subject

References

Author 安溪先生講授 *lectures delivered by him.* An Hsi Hsien Shêng ~~Chiang Shou~~

Edition Home Library
振綺堂藏 竹紙
Chên I Táng ~~Ts'ang~~ ~~block~~ Chu Chih Bamboo paper

Index 1 tao, 10 Chuan 4 tʒe

Bound in

Remarks

27

The University of Toronto Chinese Library

....

Accession No. *1227*   Index No. *149- Lg.m7*

Title   課子隨筆   *K'o Tzŭ Sui Pi*

Classification   *C -13*   *Philosophy + related subjects*

Subject   *a collection of letters, essays concerning the teaching of life + education*

References

Author   *Edited by* 張師載 (*Chang Shih Tsai*) *of the Cheng Dynasty*

Edition   *Block.* 清道光年刻   毛邊紙

樂役園藏版

Dated, Ching, Tao-Kuang Hien Ko' *period (1821-1850) "Mao-Pien" with paper*
edition—Lŏ- I-yüan 'Tsang Pan block preserved edition

Index   1

Bound in   *1 Tao,*   27卷   *4 Tsé*
          Ênh Shih Ch'i Chüan
Remarks   *27 Chüan*

50

The University of Toronto Chinese Library

. . . .

Accession No. *1228*   Index No. ~~1f~~ 030-*Lefe*

Title 問奇典註 *Wên Chi Tien Chu*

Classification *C 348 Encyclopedias*

Subject *An encyclopedia of classical terms*

References

Author 唐英 壻釋 *Explained by* *Táng, Yin Tséng* ~~Shih~~

Edition 古栢堂本 錦連係 *Ku-Po-Táng* ~~Edit.~~ *edition* "*Mien-Lien*" *paper*
~~1 Tao~~ ~~6 cb~~

Index

Bound in 1 tao 6 chuan 5 tse.

Remarks

2.

/12

The University of Toronto Chinese Library

....

Accession No. *1229*   Index No. *146-znh*

Title 西藏賦 *Hsi Tsang Fu*

Classification D 103 *Lyrics*

Subject *a lyrics on Tibet*

References

Author 清 和寧著 *Ching, Ho Ning* ~~Ctu~~

Edition *Block.* 刻寫本 ~~嘉慶年刻~~
綿連紙 ~~Ko Hsieh Pên~~ ~~Chia Ching Nien Kô~~
"*Mien-Lien*" ~~dark~~ *paper* *Tated, Chia-Ching period (1796-1820)*
edition, manuscripts

Index *None*

Bound in *1 Tao   1 tze.*

Remarks

118

The University of Toronto Chinese Library

. . . .

Accession No. *1230*   Index No. *030-9981*

Title   唐文拾遺 *Táng Wên shih yi*

Classification   *D73   Prose*

Subject   *a special collection of the essays of the Tang Dynasty.*

References

Author   *Edited by 陸心源 of the Ching Dynasty.*
              Lu Hsin-Yüan

Edition

Index   *4 tao   72 chuan   with supplementary 16 chuan. Total 27 tsie.*

Bound in

Remarks

The University of Toronto Chinese Library

....

Accession No. *1231*   Index No. 031-

Title 國朝八家四六文鈔 *Kuo Chʻao Pa Chia Ssǔ Liu Wên Chʻao*

Classification *D*

Subject

References

Author 清 吳鼒鈔 *Chʻing, Wu-Nai*

Edition 紫文閣補刊 嘉慶年刻 竹紙 *Tzǔ-Wên-Ko Pu Kan Chia Chʻing Nien Kʻo Chu Chih Bamboo paper Amended engraving edition Dated, Chia-Chʻing period (1796-1820)*

Index

Bound in 1 Tao 4 tsé

Remarks

32

48

The University of Toronto Chinese Library

. . . .

Accession No. *1232*   Index No. *172-dgdei*

Title 集說全真提要 *Chi Shuo Chüan Chên Ti yao*

Classification *C*

Subject

References

Author 清, 黃伯祿 輯, *Compiled by* *Ching, Huang Po-Lu* ~~chi~~

Edition 上海慈母堂鉛印 *Shanghai Tzŭ-Mu-Táng* *Type-setting edition* *Chien Yin*

光緒丙午年印 油光紙 夾板 *wooden folder*
Kuang ~~Shü~~ Ping Wu Nien Yin "*Yu Kuang" paper* *Chia Pan*

Index *Dated, Kuang-Hsü "Ping-Wu" 32/1906*

Bound in *1 tao   6 tsê*

Remarks

131

The University of Toronto Chinese Library
. . . .

Accession No. *1233*   Index No. *024-zabj*

Title 十七史蒙求 *Shih chi shih   Mêng chiu*

Classification *B*

Subject

References

Author 清　王逢原原著　　金三俊輯
Ch'ing,   Wang Fêng-yüan yüan chu   Compiled by Chin San-Chün

Edition 大文堂刊　　道光年刻　　白紙
Ta-Wên-Tang Edition   Tao Kuang Nien Kó   Pai Chih white paper
1 Tao   16 chuan   6 Tse
Dated, Tao-Kuang period (1821-1850)

Index

Bound in *1 tao   16 chuan   6 tse*

Remarks

132

94

The University of Toronto Chinese Library
....

Accession No. 1234   Index No. 118-adzq dd

Title 笠翁一家言全集 Li Wêng I Chia Yen Chüan Chi

Classification D 43

Subject a complete work of Mr. Li Yü (李漁) mostly essays on historical ~~accidents~~ facts.

References

Author 清李漁著 Chíng, Li Yü ~~Chu~~

Edition 芥子園版. Chieh-Tzǔ-Yüan ~~Pan~~ edition block.
竹紙 雍正八年刻 ~~Chu Ratted~~, Yung-Chêng Pa Hien Ko "Kêng-shu" 8/1730
Bamboo paper

Index

Bound in 2 tao 24 tse

Remarks see also 1300 for another version

The University of Toronto Chinese Library

....

21

Accession No. *1235*   Index No. *108-96888*

Title 盛京典制備考 *Shêng Ching Tien Chih Pei Kao*

Classification B

Subject

References

Author 清, 崇厚纂輯 *Compiled by* *Ching, Chúng Hou* ~~Fusan Chi~~

Edition

Index

Bound in   *1 tao   8 chuan   6 Tsê*

Remarks

The University of Toronto Chinese Library

....

102

Accession No. 1236   Index No. 030-chga

Title 名賢手扎 Ming Hsien Shou Cha

Classification D 43 Prose

Subject a collection of the Ching literati correspondence

References

Author Edited by 郭子瀞 Kuo Tzǔ-Ching of the Ching dynasty

Edition 湘陰郭氏岵瞻堂摹刻本 Hsiang-Yin, Kuo-Shih-Ku-Chan-Táng Hó Pên
光緒甲申年刻 綿連紙 "Mien-Lien" Chih paper
Date, Kuang-Hsü "Chia-Shên" Hien Kê
10/1884

Index

Bound in 1 tao 4 tsé

Remarks

135

The University of Toronto Chinese Library

....

76

Accession No. 1237   Index No. 170- *hgm l*

Title 陸子學譜 *Lu Tzŭ Hsüeh Pu*

Classification C

Subject

References

Author Edited by 李紱 *Li Fu* of the Ching Dynasty

Edition 無怨軒藏版 *Wu-Shu-Hsüan ~~Tsáng Pan~~ edition blocks ~~preserve~~ Preserved ed.*
雍正壬子年刊, 竹紙 夾板 *wooden folder*
Dated, Yung-chêng "gên-Tzŭ" *~~Nien Kân~~, ~~Chu Chih~~, ~~Chia Pan~~* 10/1732, *Bamboo paper*

Index

Bound in   1 tao   20 chuan 8 tsê.

Remarks

The University of Toronto Chinese Library

....

87

Accession No. *1238*   Index No. *061-egj*

Title 性理奥 *Hsing Li Ao*

Classification C-13

Subject

References

Author 明丁進篡 *Compiled by*
Ming, Ting Chin Tsuan

Edition *Block. 明刻本 竹紙*
Dated, Ming Dynastie (1643) block printed edition
Bamboo paper

Index

Bound in *1 tao. 10 Chuan 4 tsé.*

Remarks

The University of Toronto Chinese Library

· · · · · · · · · · · · · · · · · · · ·

2

Accession No. *1239*   Index No. *031-bf cj*

Title 四書合講 *Ssǔ Shu Ho Chiang*

Classification *A*

Subject

References

Author 清翁復 編次。 *edited in order by Ching, Wēng Fu Pien Tsǔ*

Edition 爱日堂刻本 毛太紙 *Ai-jih-Táng Kó-Pén edition* *"Mao tai" Chih paper*

Index

Bound in *2 tao   12 tsê.*

Remarks

138

The University of Toronto Chinese Library

. . . .

96

Accession No. *1240*   Index No. *064-mgd*

Title   擊壤集 *Chi Jang Chi*

Classification   *D*

Subject

References

Author   宋邵雍撰 *Written by Sung Shao Yung* ~~chuan~~

Edition   *Home library, Wood Block*
毛太紙   夾版
"Mao-Tai" paper ~~Chia Pan~~

Index

Bound in   *1 tao   10 chuan   6 tse*

Remarks

The University of Toronto Chinese Library

....

Accession No. *1241*　　　　Index No. *160-2hkg*

Title 辭賦標義 *Tzu Fu Piao I*

Classification *D -14*　*Elegies of Chu.*

Subject *a book on elegies.* 屈原 II 下
chü Yüan I Hsia

References

Author 　海陽俞王言阜如 著. *Hai Yang, Yü Wang Yüan, Kao Y Ju.*

Edition *Block.*

Index

Bound in *1 tao*　　　　*10 tše.*

Remarks

The University of Toronto Chinese Library

....

2

1242

Accession No. ~~1264~~   Index No. 113-mc

Title   禮記 Li Chi

Classification   A 41

Subject

References

Author   清 陳澔 集說 , *Collected by* Ching, Chên Hao ~~Chi Shao~~

Edition   浙江書局刊   光緒癸巳年刻   竹紙
Chê - Chiong-Shu Chü Kö, Kuang Shu Kwei Ssü Nienkö Chu Chih
booked. edited,   Hsü   Bamboo paper
Dated, Kuang-Hsü "Kuei-Ssü" 19/1893

Index   1 Tao   10 Chuan   10 Tse.

Bound in

Remarks

The University of Toronto Chinese Library

· ·

87

Accession No. *1243*   Index No. *072-hsg*

Title 智囊補 *Chih Nang Pu*

Classification *C. 13*

Subject *a collection of the philosophical related subjects*

References

Author 靖, 馮夢龍纂輯 *Compiled by Ching. Fêng Mêng-Lung* Tuan Chi

Edition 斐齋藏版 *Fei-Chai* Tsang Pan, *blocks preserved edition*

Index

Bound in *1 tao 28 chuan 6 tsê*

Remarks

The University of Toronto Chinese Library

....

103

Accession No. *1245*   Index No. *120-g2Ld4*

Title 佳德堂全集 *Ching Tê Táng Chüan Chi*

Classification *D*

Subject

References

Author 清 龍啓瑞撰 ~~*Written by*~~ *Ching, Lung chi-jui* ~~*Chuan*~~

Edition 家藏版 光緒四年刊 綿連紙 *"Mien Lien" ~~Chih paper~~*
~~*Chia Tsang Pan*~~ ~~*Kuang Hsü Ssü Nien Kan*~~
~~*Home Library*~~ *Dated, Kuang-Hsü "Wu-ying" 4/1878*
Private family edition

Index

Bound in 1 *tao*   21 *chuan*   10 *ts'e*

Remarks

Oct. 18, 65

46

The University of Toronto Chinese Library

. . . .

104

Accession No. *1246*   Index No. *030/bgfc*

Title 古唐詩合解 *Ku Tang Shih Ho Chieh*

Classification

Subject

References

Author 清 王堯衢註 *Annotated by Ching, Wang Yao Chü.*

Edition 致和堂刊   毛太紙 *Mao Tai paper*
Black engraving in Chih Han Tang

Index

Bound in *12 Chuan   8 tse*

Remarks

47

The University of Toronto Chinese Library
....

46

Accession No. *1247*   Index No. *030-bfgi*

Title 古品節錄 *Ku Pin Chieh Lu*

Classification 日 *117.*

Subject *a collection of short biographies of the different dynasties*

References

Author 清 松筠 撰, *Written by* *Ching, Sung Yün* ~~Chuan~~

Edition 嘉慶四年新鐫 錦連低, 延請書室藏本 *edition Tsang Pen*
~~Chia-Ching Sst Nien Hsin Chün~~ "*Mien Lien*" *paper, Yen-Ching-Shu-Wu,*
Dated, Chia-Ching "Ping-Chên" 1/1996

Index

Bound in   *1 Tao*   *6 Chuan*   *6 tsé.*

Remarks

145

The University of Toronto Chinese Library

. . . .

52

Accession No. *1248*   Index No. *020-iḡi*

Title   鮑 瓜 錄 *Páo Kua Lu*

Classification 甲 C

Subject

References

Author 明 芮長恤著 *Ming, Jui Cháng-Hsü* ~~Chu~~

Edition 家藏版   黃毛邊紙
~~Chia Tsáng Pan~~   *"Huang Mao-Pien" ~~Chih~~ paper*
~~(Home Library)~~
Private family edition.

Index

Bound in   1 *tao*   10 *Chuan*   6 *tse*.

Remarks

146

The University of Toronto Chinese Library
....

70

Accession No. *1249*   Index No. *124-eei*

Title 習是編 *Hsi Shih Pien*

Classification *C - 13*

Subject *A book on Chinese virtues.*

References

Author 清居成霖編輯 *edited & Compiled by* *Ching, Chiu Chêng-Lin Pien Chi*

Edition 家藏版 光緒年刻 竹紙夾版 *Wood-block*
Chia Tsáng Pan   Kuang Hsü Nien Kó   Chu Chih Chia Pan
Home Library   Bamboo paper
Private family edition.   Dated, Kuang-Hsü period (1875-1908)

Index *1 tao   12 chuan   4 tse*

Bound in

Remarks

147

The University of Toronto Chinese Library

. . . .

61

Accession No. *1250*   Index No. *009-Zi*

Title   人範   *Jen Fan*

Classification   *C*

Subject

References

Author   清 蔣大姶 輯 *Compiled by* *ching, Chiang Ta-Shih chi*

Edition   家藏版 ~~Library~~ 棼 版 *"Fên" chih paper*
Private family edition

Index

Bound in   1 *tao*   6 *chuan*   4 *ts'e*

Remarks

The University of Toronto Chinese Library
. . . .

58

Accession No.   *1-257/*   Index No. *036-友ゐ友*

Title   夢溪筆談   *Mêng Hsi Pi Tán*

Classification   *C-308.*

Subject   *A collection of miscellaneous writing on different subject.*

References   宋 沈括撰, ^{*Written by*} *Sung, Shên Kuo* ~~Chuan~~

Author   ↗

Edition   番禺(Canton) 陶氏愛廬校刊   *Fan-Yü*   *Táo Shih Ai Lu,*
光緒三十二年刻 綿連紙 夾版   ~~*Hsiao Kan*~~ *Wood-block*   ^{*Collated ed.*}
Dated, Kuang-Hsü ~~*San Shih*~~ *Nien Ko "Mien Lien" paper* ~~*Chia Pan*~~
Index   *"Ping-Wu" 32/1906*

Bound in   1 *tao*   26 *Chuan*   4 *tse.*

Remarks

The University of Toronto Chinese Library
. . . .

35ʹ

Accession No. 1252   Index No. 031-bgicdalfie
                                      031-bgicdalfc

Title 四庫湖北先正遺書題要 四庫湖北先正遺書存目
      Ssŭ Kü Hu Pei Hsien Chêng I Shu Ti yao Ssŭ Kü Hu Pei Hsien Chêng I Shu Tsün Mu

Classification B-342

Subject a general summary of Chinese classics.

References

Author 清 盧 靖 輯刊   Compiled + block engraved by
                        Ching, Lu Ching Chi Kan

Edition 盧氏 Home library 家藏版 Private family edition.
        Lu-Shih

         綿連紙 夾版 Wood-block
        "Mien-Lien" paper Piet Chia Pan

Index 1

Bound in 1 tao 8 chuan 4 tse.

Remarks

The University of Toronto Chinese Library

. . . .

22

Accession No.   *1253*   Index No. *077-lcbf*

Title   歷代史畧 *Li Tai Shih Lüeh*

Classification   B

Subject

References

Author

Edition   江楚書局列 *Chiang-Chu* *book co. edition* *Shu Chü Kän*
毛邊紙 翻版 *"Mao-Pien" Chih* *Chia Pan*
paper
wooden folder

Index

Bound in   2 *tao*   6 *chuan*   8 *tse*

Remarks

The University of Toronto Chinese Library
. . . .

68

Accession No.   *1254*   Index No. *212 Hil*

Title   龍文鞭影 *Lung Wên Pien Ying*

Classification   *C - 13*

Subject   *a classical book of a quadrdlateral arrangement (o4-characters classics) on Chinese litival, historical terms.*

References

Author   明蕭良有著 *Ming, Hsiao Liang-Yu Chu*

Edition   道光年刊, 毛邊紙 夾版 *Wood-block wooden-folder* *Dated, Tao-Kuang Nien Kan "Mao Pien Edit period (1821-1850) paper Chia Pan*

Index

Bound in   *1 tao   2 Chuan   4 tsé*

Remarks

152

95

Accession No. 1255   Index No. 067-3333

Title 文章指南 Wên Chang Chih Nan

Classification D73 Prose

Subject A general collection of Chinese
classical proses written by leading
literati of different period & with
comments by Kwei Yu Kwang of the
References Ming Dynasty.

Author 明 歸有光 選   清 許筱蓮 輯
Selected by Ming, Kwei Yu-Kuang Compiled of Ching, Hsü Hsiao-Lien Chi
Edition 皖江節署校刊 Huan-Chiang, Chieh-Shu Hsiao Kan revised edition
黃毛太紙   光緒二年刊   夾版 Wood-block
"Huang Mao Tai Chih   Kuang Hsü Ênh Nien Kan   Chia Pan
paper
Index Dated, Kuang-Hsü "Ping-Tzŭ" 2/1876

Bound in 1 tao   5 tse.

Remarks

153

The University of Toronto Chinese Library

. . . .

60

Accession No.   *1256*   Index No. *074-hdjc*

Title   朝野雜記 *Chao Yeh Tsa Chi*

Classification   C

Subject

References

Author   宋 李心傳撰 *Written by* *Sung, Li Hsin-Ch'uan Chuan*

Edition   光緒癸巳年刊 錦連係 *Dated* *Kuang-Hsü "Kuei-Ssŭ" Nien Kan 19/1893* *"Mien-Lien" Chih paper*
井研蓋氏刊本 *Ching-Yen, Lu Shih Kan Pen edition block-printing edition*

Index

Bound in   1 t'ao   40 chuan   12 ts'e.

Remarks

154

43

Accession No. _1257_   Index No. 201-引引从

Title 黃巖西橋王氏譜 *Huang Yen Hsi Chiao Wang Shih Pu*

Classification β

Subject

References

Author 清   王舟瑤纂 *Compiled by* *Ching, Wang Chou-Yao* ~~Editor~~

Edition 聚珍板印 白竹紙 夾裝 ~~Weed-block~~ *wooden-folder*
Chu Chen Pan Yin Pai Chu Chih Chia Pan Movable-type edition
White bamboo paper

Index

Bound in   1 tao   12 chuan 附家集十卷.   12 tse.

Remarks

155

. . . .

97

Accession No. *1258*   Index No. *024-ghghd*

Title 南華經箋註 *Nan Hua Ching Chien Chu*

Classification *C - 513*

Subject

References

Author 釋性通註 *Shih Hsing-Tung annotations*

Edition 雲林懷德堂梓行 *Yüan-Lin, Huai-Tê-Tang Tyü Hsing*
毛邊紙 *"Mao-Pien" Chih paper*

Index

Bound in *1 tao   8 chuan   6 tsê*

Remarks

The University of Toronto Chinese Library

. . . .

23

Accession No. 1259   Index No. 115-jb釗九

Title 稽古錄 Chi Ku Lu

Classification B 22 other unclassified histories.

Subject A history of China from the early days to the Sung Dynasty by Ssŭ Ma Kwang.

References

Author 宋,司馬光撰。 *Written by* Sung, Ssŭ-Ma Kuang (~~Chuan~~)

Edition 崇文書局版. Chung-Wên Shu Chü *book co. edition* ~~Pan~~

同治十一年刻, 粉紙 夾板 提鄉藏 *preserved*
Dated, Tüng-Chih Shih I Nien Kʻo, "fên" Chih Chia Pan Chi Ching ~~Tsang~~ *edition*
"gên-Shen" 11/1872 *paper* *wood block*

Index 1 一

Bound in 1 tao   20 chuan   4 tsé.

Remarks

157

The University of Toronto Chinese Library

....

//

Accession No. *1260*   Index No. *030-ede*~~x~~

Title 周易費氏學 *Chou I fei Shih Hsüeh*

Classification *A — //*

Subject A *series of* commentary lectures on the Book of Changes

References

Author 馬其永旦 撰 *Written by* *Ma C'hi Cháng* ~~Chuan~~

Edition 豫章饒氏等刊 *Yü-Chang-gao Shih* ~~Fêng Kan~~ *and others* block engraving
龍門紙夾板 *"Lung Mên" Chih paper Chia Pan Wood-block*

Index *1 tao 8 Chuan 4 t'se,*
↑

Bound in

Remarks

The University of Toronto Chinese Library

. . . .

108

Accession No. *1261*   Index No. *040-9 聞*

Title 宮閨文選 *Kung Kuei Wên Hsüan*

Classification *D 63*

Subject *a collection of essays, lyrics, poems*
+c by women of the different dynasties

References

Author 清 周壽昌 *Ching, Chou Shou-Chang*   *blak preserved*
                                              edition
Edition 小蓬萊山館藏版 *Hsiao-Pêng-Lai Shan-Kuan* ^*Tsang Pan*
道光年刻 白竹紙 夾版 *Wooden folder*
Dated, Tao-Kuang Nien-Ko Pai Chu Chih   Chia Pan
           period (1821-1850) white bamboo paper

Index

Bound in   1 *tao*   十九卷（附錄二卷. 詩楷二卷）. 14 *tse*

Remarks

159

The University of Toronto Chinese Library

· ·

Accession No. ~~1772~~ 1262   Index No. 030·229

Title 呻吟語 Shên Yin Yü

Classification C — ~~308~~ 鬼怪器 — 韓社
              13

Subject *It divides into two general ~~topic~~ sections.*
First section — individual ethic + personality.
Second " — The relation of individual to
the community.

References

Author 明. 宁坤著 (Ming) Lü Kún

Edition 明 宁坤原板, 白毛边纸印
        Ming, Wan-Li period edition (1593-1619), white "Mao-Pien" paper

Index *a general table of contents for 6 chüan* —

Bound in *1 t'ao, 6 chüan,* + 封 t'ao

Remarks

Cab. I

The University of Toronto Chinese Library
66
....

Accession No.   1262   Index No. 030-edq

Title   呻吟語 Shên Yin Yü

Classification C 13   Philosophy & related subject

Subject A book on Chinese personal morality
& human relationship

References

Author 明呂坤著 Ming, Lü Kún

Edition 松茂堂藏版 Sung-Mao-Tang (Tsáng Pan) block preserved.
同治年刻 Tung-Chih (Nien-Kò) period (1862-1874)
綿連紙 "Mien-Lien" (Chih) paper

Index 1

Bound in 1 tao 12 chuan 6 tse.

Remarks

The University of Toronto Chinese Library

. . . .

43

Accession No.   1263   Index No. 162 - ija b

Title   道齊正軌 *Tao Chi Chêng Kuei*

Classification   B 117   collected biographies

Subject   a collection of Chinese officials' biographies from the Chou to the Ming Dynasties.

References

Author   Edited by 鄒鳴鶴 *Tsou Ming-Ho*

Edition   ~~Home library~~   道光二十三年刻 *Tao Kuang Êrh Shih San Nien Kó* 竹紙 ~~Chu Chih~~ Dated, *Too-Kuang "Kuei-Mao" 23 / 1843* Bamboo paper

Index   家藏版 *Private family edition*

Bound in   1 *tao*   30 *Chuan*   8 *tse*

Remarks

162

The University of Toronto Chinese Library

....

13

Accession No. *1264* ~~1542~~   Index No. *113—MC*

Title 禮記 *Li chi*

Classification *A*

Subject

References

Author

Edition 江西書局刊, 同治十三年刻 綿連紙

夾版 Wood-block   *"Chia-Hsü" 13/1874*   *"Nien Lien")*

Chiang-Hsi Book Company ~~Dated~~, *Tung-Chih Shih San Nien Ho,*   *(Paper*

Index ~~Chih~~ ~~Chia Pan~~

Bound in   *1 tao   10 Chuan   10 ts'e.*

Remarks

163

The University of Toronto Chinese Library

· ·

12

Accession No.   *1265*   Index No. *149-fi*

Title   詩牽 *Shih Chi*

Classification   *A 31   Book of Poetry*

Subject

References

Author   宋, 嚴粲述 ~ *Given in oral by* *Sung, Yen Tsan Shu*

Edition   雜園重校刊本 *Sui-Yüan ~~Chung Hsiao Kan Pen~~ revised edition collated edition*
          光緒庚寅年刊 *Dated: Kuang-Hsü "Kêng-Yin" Nien Kan 16/1890*
          毛邊紙 *"Mao Pien" Shih paper*

Index

Bound in   *2 tao   36 Chuan   12 tse.*

Remarks

164

The University of Toronto Chinese Library

· ·

103

<u>Accession No.</u> 1266   <u>Index No.</u> 018-egbj#

<u>Title</u>   初唐四傑集 Ch'u Tang Ssŭ Chieh Chi

<u>Classification</u>   D

<u>Subject</u>

<u>References</u>

<u>Author</u> 唐　王勃 等著 Tang, Wang Po Teng Chu
                                    and others

<u>Edition</u> 星渚項氏校刊 Hsing-Chu, Hsiang Shih Hsiao Kan
                                    shih revised edition
                                          collated

<u>Index</u>

<u>Bound in</u>   1 tao   12 tsê

<u>Remarks</u>

The University of Toronto Chinese Library

· · · · · · · · · · · · · · · · · · · ·

98

Accession No. *1267*   Index No. *075-fdz*

Title   桃花扇 *Táo Hua Shan*

Classification   D

Subject

References

Author   雲亭山人 編 *edited by* „ *Yün-Tíng-Shan-jên Pien collated re—Revised edition*

Edition   蘭雪堂重校刊本 *Lan-Hsüeh-Táng Chúng Hsiao Kán Pên*

Index

Bound in   *1 tao   5 chuan   5 ts̆e*

Remarks

The University of Toronto Chinese Library

....

39

Accession No. *1268*   Index No. *149-0 b k u*

Title 讀史漫錄 *Tu Shih Man Lu*

Classification *B*

Subject

References

Author 清 于慎行著 *Ching, Yü Shên-Hsing Chu*

Edition 存素齋存版 *Tsun-Su-Chai Tsun Pan preserved edition.*
道光年刻 錦連依 夾版 *Woodan block folder*
Tao Kuang Nien Kô "Mien Lien" Chih Chia Pan
paper

Index *Dated, Tao-Kuang period (1821—1850)*

Bound in *1 tao   20 chuan   10 tsê.*

Remarks

The University of Toronto Chinese Library
. . . .

122

Accession No. *1269*   Index No. 149- *dzh bt td*

Title 許文肅公外集 *Hsü Wên Su Kung Wai Chi*

Classification *D*

Subject

References

Author 清 許景澄 著 | 盛 沅 編輯 *compiled + edited by*
Ching Hsü Ching-Chêng Chu √Shêng Yüan Pien Chi

Edition 鉛印本 *Chien Yin Pên Type-setting edition*
連史紙 "*Lien-shih*" *Chih paper*

Index   1 tao   5 chuan   4 tse.

Bound in

Remarks

168

The University of Toronto Chinese Library

· ·

70

Accession No. *1270*   Index No. *198 zdg b※*

Title 鹿忠節公集 *Lu Chung Chieh Kung Chi*

Classification *D*

Subject

References

Author 清 鹿善繼著 *Ching, Lu Shan-Chi* ~~Chu~~

Edition ~~Home library~~ 家藏版 *Private family edition*

Index

Bound in 1 *tao* 21 *chuan* 6 *tsê*

Remarks

The University of Toronto Chinese Library

. . . .

58

Accession No.   1291   Index No. 031-b7bg

Title   四書反身錄 Ssǔ Shu Fan Shěn Lu

Classification   C - 13   Philosophy & related subjects

Subject   A book on the recollection & influence
of Confucian 4 books on morality.

References

Author   清 李容著 Ching, Li Jung Chu

Edition   三韓劉氏版 San Han, Liu-Shih Fan blocks
竹紙 Chu Chih Bamboo paper

Index

Bound in   1 tao   8 chuan   4 tsé

Remarks

5

Accession No.   1292   Index No. 067 gc b j ty

Title   文字求蒙廣義 Wên Tzǔ Chiu Mêng Kuan I

Classification   A

Subject

References

Author   明方應祥纂 Compiled by
          Ming, Fang Ying-Hsiang Tsuan

Edition   明刻本,竹紙 Ming Kʻo Pên, Chu Chih,
                        Bamboo paper
                 Dynasty (1368 - 1643)

Index

Bound in   1 tao   4 tsé

Remarks

29

The University of Toronto Chinese Library
....

Accession No. *1273*   Index No. *072.db99*

Title   明史例案 *Ming shih Li An*

Classification   *B*

Subject

References

Author   劉承幹纂 *Compiled by Liu Chêng-Kan* ~~Trust~~

Edition   吳興劉氏嘉業堂刊 *Wu-Hsing, Liu shih, Chai-Yeh Tang* *edited* ~~Kau~~

Index

Bound in   *1 tao   9 chuan   4 tse.*

Remarks

√ 74

The University of Toronto Chinese Library
....

45

Accession No. 1274   Index No. 040-dhaithth

Title 宋陳火陽先生盡忠錄 Sung Chên Shao Yang Hsien Shêng Chin
                                    Chung Lu

Classification B-107

Subject

References

Author

Edition 抄寫精本 manuscript copy
                    Chao Hsieh Ching-Pên
        毛邊紙 "Mao-Pien" Chih paper

Index

Bound in 1 tao 8 Chuan 2 tse

Remarks

173

The University of Toronto Chinese Library

. . . .

33

Accession No. *1295*   Index No. *072-d611*

Title 明史例案 Ming Shih Li An

Classification *B*

Subject

References

Author 劉承幹纂, *Compiled by Liu Chêng-Kan* ~~Tsun~~

Edition 劉氏家業堂刊 *Liu Shih, Chai-Yeh Tang* ~~Kan~~ *edited block-engraving.*

Index 1

Bound in 1 *tao*   9 *chuan*   4 *tsê*

Remarks

The University of Toronto Chinese Library

. . . .

Accession No. **1276**   Index No. 140-乂*z*

Title 萬言肆雅 Wan Yen I Ya

Classification A 61   Graphic dictionaries

Subject · a book of 10 thousand characters arranging in 8 character sentences with comments & notes, oo too

References

Author 清, 屈曹發撰 *Written by* Ching, Chiu Tséng Fa ~~Chuan~~

Edition 宗園藏版 I-Yuan ~~Tsang Pan~~ *edition* block preserved.

同治庚午年重刻本 綿連紙 夾板 *wooden-folder.*

Dated, Tung-Chih "Kéng-Wu" Nien Chung Ko Pén "Mien Lien" Chih Chia Pan

Index *9/1870 re-printed paper* ~~Wood-block~~

Bound in   1 tao   6 tsé

Remarks

The University of Toronto Chinese Library
. . . .

63

Accession No. ,277   Index No. 140.喜

Title 莊子雪 *Chuang Tzŭ Hsüeh*

Classification C 303

Subject a complete work of 莊子
with notes & biography

References

Author 清 陸樹芝輯註, Ching, Lu Shu-Chih *Chi-Chu* *Compiled & annotated by*

Edition 粵東儒雅堂版 Yüeh-Tung, Ju-Ya-Tang *edition blocks*

Index

Bound in 1 tao 3 chuan 6 tse

Remarks

176

The University of Toronto Chinese Library

7

....

Accession No.   1298   Index No. 040-de i a

Title   宋紹熙本公羊傳注 Sung Shao Hsi Pên Kung Yang Chuan Chu

Classification   A

Subject

References

Author   游

Edition   清 汪喜孫等重校刊本 Ching, Wang Hsi-Sun
                                                 Kung Pên
            re-collated
            re-revised edition
            and other Têng Chung Hsiao
          道光四年刊   毛邊紙
          Dated, Tao-Kúng Ssŭ Nien Kan   "Mao-Pien" Chik paper
Index   "Chia-Shen" 4/1824

Bound in   1 tao   12 chuan   2 tse

Remarks

The University of Toronto Chinese Library

....

121

Accession No. *1279*   Index No. *085-chepd*

Title 江漢炳靈集 *Chiang Han Ping Ling Chi*

Classification *D*

Subject

References

Author 清，張之洞輯 *Compiled by* *Ching, Chang Chih-Tung Chi*

Edition 官版 *Official Copy* *Kuan Pan*   同治九年刻 *Tung Chih Chia Nien Ko* 連史紙 *"Lien Shih Chih" paper* 夾版 *Chia Pan* *Wooden block folder*
Dated, Tung-Chih "Keng-Wu" 9/1870

Index

Bound in   1 *tao*   2 *Chuan*   4 *tse.*

Remarks

178

The University of Toronto Chinese Library

. . . .

22

Accession No.   1281   Index No. 120.02c

Title   續漢志   Hsü Han Chih

Classification   B-137

Subject

References

Author   梁劉昭註補   Amended Annotation by Liang Liu Chao Chu Pu

Edition   浙江書局刊   毛邊紙
Chieh-Chiang-Shu-Chü Kan   Mao-Pien Chih paper
book co.   edited   blocks-engraving .

Index   1

Bound in   1 tao   30 chuan   2 ts'e

Remarks

The University of Toronto Chinese Library

. . . .

100

Accession No. *1282*   Index No. 060-_{處集}

Title 御製文初集 *Yü chih Wên Ch'u Chi*

Classification D 43   *Prose*

Subject *a collection of essays concerning political & moral issues, also some long imperial edicts & praises.*

References

Author 清道光帝撰, *Written by Ch'ing, Tao Kuang, Emperor Ti Chuan*

Edition 殿版 單宣紙 夾版 *Wooden block folder.*
Tien Pan "Tan-Hsuan Chih Chia Pan
Palace edition   paper

Index

Bound in   *1 tao   5 tse*

Remarks

83

The University of Toronto Chinese Library

. . . .

85

Accession No.   1283   Index No.   007-bild

Title   五種遺規 Wu Chung I Kuei

Classification   C-329

Subject

References   Toronto No. 960, 961

Author   清 陳宏謀 編輯 Ching, Chén Hung-Mou
                      edited & Compiled by

Edition   金陵書局重刊 同治年刻 竹紙
          Chin Ling Shu Chü Chung Kan, Tung Chih Nien Ko   Chu Chih
                    reprinted edition,   Bamboo paper
          Dated, Tung-Chih period (1862-1874)

Index

Bound in   2 tao   17 Chuan   10 Tse.

Remarks

181

The University of Toronto Chinese Library

. . . .

40

Accession No. _1284_   Index No. _169-遜_

Title 闕里述聞 *Chüeh Li Shu Wên*

Classification B

Subject

References

Author 清 鄭曉如 敬述 *Gwên ein oral by*
Ching, Chêng Hsiao-ju ~~Ching Shu~~

Edition 西湖華文堂刊 *Hsi-Hu, Hua-Wên-Táng* *edition* ~~han edited~~ *blocks.*

Index

Bound in   1 *tao*   14 *chuan*   8 *tsê*

Remarks

The University of Toronto Chinese Library

. . . .

Accession No. 81 1285   Index No. 0503gn

Title 巾経纂 Chin Ching Tsuan

Classification C328 Extracts from various
works compiled & edited

Subject The collection of essays thus historic
accounts illustrating political
wisdom & tactfulness.

References

Author 清 宋宗元著 Ching, Sung Tsung-Yüan chu

Edition 嘉孚堂刊本 Chia-Fu-Táng Kan Pên block-print edition
感豊五年刊 竹紙 Hsien Fêng Wu Nien Kan Cha Chih
Bamboo paper

Index Dated, Hsien-Fêng "I-Mao" 5/1855

Bound in 1 tao 20 Chuan 5 tʻse

Remarks

The University of Toronto Chinese Library

. . . .

119

Accession No. *1286*   Index No. *075-c 斜*

Title 李義山詩集 *Li I Shan Shih Chi*

Classification D38 *Verse*

Subject

References

Author 唐李義山 *Táng, Li I-Shan*   *commentaried &*
                                                    printed in five
Edition 精刻本 五色批點 *Ching Kó Pên   Wu Sê Pi Tien*
         Fine-printed edition,

         順治年刻 綿連紙 *Shun Chih Nien Kó   "Mien Lien" chih*
                                                          paper
         Dated, Shun-Chih period (1653→1661)

Index

Bound in   1 *tao*   3 *chuan*   3 *tśe*

Remarks

The University of Toronto Chinese Library

....

Accession No. 1287   Index No. 040-不易
075-R8
085-cedg

Title 寤言 二卷 權制 八卷 江表忠畧 二十卷
Wu Yen 二卷 Chüan Chih 八卷 Chiang Piao Chung Lüch 二十卷

Classification B72 Memorials, petitions &c.

Subject a series of political essays
on various subjects.

References

Author 陳澹然著 Chên Tan-jan chu

Edition

Index

Bound in 1 tao

Remarks   12 tse

185

The University of Toronto Chinese Library

....

103

Accession No. *1288*   Index No. *061-hecd*

Title 惜抱軒全集 *Hsi Pao Hsüan Chüan Chi*

Classification *D*

Subject

References

Author 清 姚鼐 撰 *Written by* *Ching, Yao Nai* ~~Chuan~~

Edition ~~Home library~~ 家藏版 *Private family edition*
竹紙 夾版 *Wooden folder*
Chu Chih Chia Pan
Bamboo paper

Index

Bound in   1 *tao*   26 *chuan*   6 *tse*

Remarks

The University of Toronto Chinese Library

. . . .

30

Accession No.　1289　　　　Index No. 167.c...　338.

Title　金石文字辨異補編　Ching Shih Wên Tzŭ Pien I Pu Pien

Classification　B

Subject

References

Author　清 楊紹廉 撰。 Written by Ching, Yang Shao-Lien ~~Chuan~~

Edition　寫印本 Hsieh Yin Pên Manuscript Copy
毛邊紙 "Mao-Pien" ~~Cloth~~ paper

Index

Bound in　　　5 tsê

Remarks

187

83

Accession No. *1290*   Index No. *149-07jm*

Title 讀書雜釋 *Tu Shu Tsa Shih*

Classification C

Subject

References

Author 清 徐鼎鑅 *Compiled by* *Ching, Hsü Ting Tsuan*

Edition 福寧郡齋藏版 *Fu-Ning, Chün-Chai Tsang Pan* *block preserved.*
咸豐年刻 綿連紙 夾版 *Wood block woaden-folder*
Dated, Hsien-Fêng Nien K'o "Mien Lien Chih Chia Pan
Index   *period (1851-1861) paper*

Bound in   1 tao   14 Chuan   4 tsé

Remarks

90

188

The University of Toronto Chinese Library

. . . .

34

Accession No. _1291_   Index No. _109-cc ḡ i ḡi_

Title 直齋書錄解題 _Chih Chai Shu Lu Chieh Ti_

Classification B. 342 _Books & writings in general_

Subject _a catalogues of all kinds of books & writings_

References

Author 宋. 陳振孫 撰 _Written by_ _Sung, Chên Chên-Sun Chuan_

Edition 江蘇書局列 _Chiang-Su-Shu-Chü Kan_ _book co., edited_
光緒九年刻 綿連紙
Dated, Kuang-Hsü Chiu Nien Kó "Mien Lien" Chih paper
"Kuei-Wei" 9/1883

Index

Bound in 1 tao 22 Chuan 6 tsè

Remarks

The University of Toronto Chinese Library

. . . .

101

Accession No. *1292*

Index No. *061-hectz*

Title 惜抱軒文集 *Hsi Pao Hsüan Wên Chi*

Classification *D*

Subject

References

Author 清姚鼐 *Ching, Yao Nai*

Edition 桐城徐氏重校刊本 *Tung-Chêng, Hsü Shih Chuan Hsiao Kan Pên* ~~re-issued edition~~ re-collated edition

光緒癸未年刊 綿連紙 夾版 *Wooden ~~block~~ folder*

Dated, Kuang-Hsü "Kuei-Wei" Nien Kan "Mien Lien Chih" Chia Pan paper

9/1883

Index

Bound in 1 *tao* 16 *chuan* 4 *t'se*

Remarks

190

The University of Toronto Chinese Library

....

26

Accession No. 1293   Index No. 030-bceg

Title 史記狐白 Shih Chi Hu Pai

Classification B 詩 12   official Dynastic Histories

Subject ~~Another version of~~ a Ming Dynasty version of Shih Chih.

References

Author 明 湯賓尹精選 Fine selected by Ming, Táng Pin-Yin ~~Ching Hsüan~~

Edition 明刻本 竹紙
Dated, Ming Ko Pen edition Dynasty   Chu Chih bamboo paper
Ming block print (1368-1643)

Index

Bound in 1 tao 6 chuan 6 Tse

Remarks

The University of Toronto Chinese Library

. . . .

Accession No. *1294*   Index No. *180zj*

Title 音 韻 註署 約編   *Yin Yün*   *Chu Lüeh*
                                      Yüeh Pien

Classification   *A*

Subject

References

Author 清, 張彭緒 *Ching, Chang Pêng-Hsü*

Edition 家藏版, *Chia Tsang Pan Home Library Private family edition*
咸豐元年刊 葆真堂藏版 *Pao-Chên-Tang edition block preserved*
Hsien Fêng Yüen Nien Kan edition
白毛太紙 *"Pai-Mao-Tai" Chih paper*

Index *Dated, Hsien-Fêng "Hsing-Hai" 1/1851*

Bound in   1 *tao*   4 *tsê*

Remarks

The University of Toronto Chinese Library
....

23

Accession No. _1295_   Index No. 030-bcd

Title   史記抄 _Shih Chi Chào_

Classification   B

Subject

References

Author   明茅坤 抄 *manuscripted by* *Ming, Mao Kún* ~~Chao~~

Edition   明萬曆乙亥年精刻本 *Ming Wan-Li I Hai Nien Ching Ko Pén* *Fine-printed edition*
明白綿紙　夾板 *Ming,* *Dynasty, "Pai-Mien" Chih paper* *Chia Pan. Wooden block folder*
Dated, Ming, Wan-Li "I-Hai" 3//1575

Index

Bound in   = Tao 91 Chüan 24 _tsé_

Remarks

The University of Toronto Chinese Library
. . . .

5

Accession No.   1297   Index No. 149-g²/k a

Title   說文聲系 *Shuo Wên Shêng Hsi*

Classification   A

Subject

References

Author   清 姚文田撰 *Written by Chîng, Yao Wên-Tien*

Edition   粵東督學使署刻 *Yüeh-Tung, Tu-Hsüeh-Shih-Shu-Kô*

嘉慶甲子年刻. 連史紙 *Dated, Chia-Chîng "Chia Tzu" "Nien Kô "Lien Shih" Chih paper 9/1804*

Index

Bound in   1 tao   2 tsê

Remarks

194

The University of Toronto Chinese Library

. . . .

40

Accession No. *1298*   Index No. 060-*h1 ze got*

Title 御撰資治通鑑綱目 *Yü Chuan Tzŭ Chih Tung Chien Kang Mu*

Classification *B*

Subject

References

Author *Edited by* 清張廷玉 &C. *Ching, Chang Ting-yü*

Edition 殿版   開化紙 *Tien Pan. "Kai-Hua" Chih paper*
乾隆十一年刻有硃印玉璽 *printed in red*
Dated, Chien-Lung Shih I Nien Kó Yu Chu Yin Yü Hsi

Index   *"Ping-Yin" 11/1946*

Bound in   *1 tao   20 chuan   4 tśe*

Remarks

The University of Toronto Chinese Library
. . . .

107

Accession No.   *1299*   Index No. 030-ξdb

Title 周文忠公尺牘 *Chou Wên Chung Kung Chih Tu*

Classification *D*

Subject

References

Author 鄞松靖, 周天爵 著 *Ching, Chou Tien-Chüeh*

Edition 蘇松太道署刊   同治年刻 *Dated Su-Sung Tai-Tao Shu Kan blocks*
        綿連紙 *"Mien-Lien" paper. Chih*

Index *Dated, Tung-Chih period (1862-1874)*

Bound in *1 tao   2 tse*

Remarks

100

The University of Toronto Chinese Library

....

100

Accession No.　1300　　　　Index No. 118-edg世

Title　笠翁一家言全集 Li Wêng I Chia Yen Chüan Chi

Classification　D 43

Subject　A complete work of Mr. Li Yu
chiefly essays on historical facts.

References

Author　清　李漁　撰　Written by Ching, Li Yü 撰

Edition　芥子園藏版　Chieh-Tzŭ-Yüan Tsang Pan blocks preserved.
Bamboo paper

Index　2 tao　　16 Chuan　　20 tsé

Bound in

Remarks　There are two versions　see 1234

. . . .

13

Accession No. *1301*   Index No. *073 - f9*

Title   書 經 *Shu Ching*

Classification *A - 21*

Subject

References

Author

Edition   江 西 書 局 刊, *Chiang-shi shu Chü Kǎn* *book co. edited*
          同治十三年刻 *(mien-hing paper)*
          木版. *Tùng Chih shih san Nien K'o)*

Index   *Chi̧a̧ Pan*   *Chia Pan Dated: Tùng-Chih "Chia-Hsü" 13/1874*
                      Wood-block

Bound in   *1 tao   10 chuan   10 tsě.*

Remarks

198

The University of Toronto Chinese Library

....

13

Accession No. *1302*   Index No. *072-edk*

Title 春秋左傳 *Chūn Chiu Tso Chuan*

Classification   *A 101*

Subject

References

Author 宋岳珂刊補 *Sung, Ya Kó Kán Pu* *Yüeh ? engraver.*

Edition 江西書局刊 *Chiang-shi Shu Chü Kán* *book Co.*
同治十三年刻 *(Mien-hien paper)*
(Tung Chih Shih San Nien Kó)
夾版 *Chia Pan* *Chia Pan Wood-block*

Index *Dated, Tung-Chih "Chia-Hsü" 13/1874*

Bound in *2 táo 30 Chuan 16 tsé.*

Remarks

199

The University of Toronto Chinese Library

．．．．．．．．．．．．．．．．．．．．．

I think I must have found this

29

Accession No. *1303*   Index No. *210-zi*

Title 齊 乘 ~~Chiai~~ *Chêng*
                    Chʻi

Classification *B*
                     -192

Subject

References

Author 明 于 欽 纂 *compiler, edit Ming, Yü-Chʻin* ~~Tsuan~~

Edition *re cut of Ming edition* 明刊本，竹紙 夾版 *Ming Pan Pên*
          actually chʻien-lung period *Chu Chih Bamboo paper*
                                        Chia Pan Wood-block

Index *Dated. Ming, Dynastie (1368—1643)*

Bound in   *1 tao   6 chuan   6 tsě*

Remarks

The University of Toronto Chinese Library

. . . .

73

Accession No. 1304   Index No. 170-fgPc

Title 陔餘叢攷 Kai Yü Ts'ung K'ao

Classification   C 308   雜文 Tsa Wên

Subject a collection of miscellaneous writings
discussions on classical & historical
subjects by Chao I

References

Author Chao I of the Ch'ing Dynasty 清, 趙翼

Edition 湛貽堂藏 版 Chan-I-Tang Ts'ang Pan
乾隆年刻 竹紙 夾板 Chien Lung Nien k'o
Bamboo paper Chia Pan Chu Chih
Wood-block   Chia Pan
Index   Dated, Chien-Lung period (1736-1795)

Bound in 1 tao 40 chuan 14 ts'e

Remarks

Japan - Relations with the west

```
Japan
  952  Williams, Harold S
  Wil    Tales of the foreign settlements
         in Japan ... decorations by Jean
         Willaims.  Tokyo, Rutland, Tuttle
         1958

         351 p.  illus., plates
```

The University of Toronto Chinese Library

....

112

Accession No. 1305   Index No. 075 — 2 ij9

Title   松陽講義 Sung Yáng Chiang I

Classification   C- 13

Subject   An exposition on every chapter of the four Books. It is written in a plain Madarin literary style.

References

Author   清 陸隴其著 Ching, Lu Lung Chai Chu

Edition   固始張氏重刊 光緒年刻, Ku-Shih Chang Shih Chúng Kan Hsü
Ku-Shih, Chang Shih re-edited
硃印 (red print) Chu Ying
綿連紙 "Mien-lien" paper Shih
Dated, Kuang-Hsü period (1875—1908)

Index

Bound in   1 tao   12 Chuan   6 tse

Remarks

The University of Toronto Chinese Library

. . . .

125

Accession No. *1306*   Index No. *140-j王身fW*

Title   蒙養正書二編 *Mêng Yang Hên Shu San Pien*

Classification   *C -338*

Subject

References

Author   清張永變纂 *Ch'ing, Chang Ch'êng Hsieh Tsuan*

Edition   東館兩堂刊本 *Tung-Ting Liang T'ang* ~~Kên Pên~~ *Block-printed Pên*

Index   *1*

Bound in   *1 t'ao   12 ts'ê*

Remarks

The University of Toronto Chinese Library
. . . .

Accession No. *49* 1307   Index No. 030—*чjk*

Title 古今類傳 *Ku Chin Lei Chüan*

Classification C

Subject

References

Author 清, 黃穀士輯 *Ch'ing, Huang Ku-shih Chi*

Edition *Home Library Edition.*
(Bamboo paper)
竹 紙   *Chu Chih*

Index

Bound in *1 tao   4 Chuan   4 Tse.*

Remarks

The University of Toronto Chinese Library

. . . .

56

Accession No.   1308   Index No. 096— 8733 李商隐

Title   玉谿生詩詳註 *Yü Chi shêng Shih Hsiang Chu*

Classification

Subject

References

Author ① 唐 李商隱 著. ② 清 馮孟亭 編 訂

Edition ③ 德聚堂藏版   ① *Tâng, Li Shang-yin st Chu*
　　　 ④ 連莊藏 白紙.   ② *Ching, Fêng Mêng-Ting Pien Ting*
　　　　　　　　　　　　 ③ *Tê-Chü-Tâng Tsâng Pan edition*
Index　　　　　　　　　 ④ *Ti-Chuang Tsâng   Pai Chih*
　　　　　　　　　　　　　　　　 edited   *White paper*

Bound in   1 tao   3 chuan   4 tse.

Remarks

206

The University of Toronto Chinese Library
....

97

Accession No. *1309*   Index No. *195 — Chi fhqd*

Title 鮚埼皮亭集 *Chi Chi Ting Chi*

Classification *D*

Subject

References

Author 清 全祖望著 *Ching, Chüan Tsu-Wang Chu*

Edition 借樹山房版 *Chieh-Shu-Shan-Fang* edition
毛邊紙　　二夾版 *"Mao-Pien" Chih Êrh Chia Pan*
Double Wood-block

Index

Bound in　*2 tao　38 chuan　32 tse.*

Remarks

The University of Toronto Chinese Library

....

Accession No. 1310   Index No. 037 — fmmc

Title 奎壁禮記 K'uei Pi Li Chi

Classification A 41

Subject

References

Author 清 陳澔集說 Ching, Chén Hao-Chi shuo

Edition 善成堂藏版 正韻字体 Shan-Chéng-Tang Tsang Pam edition
光緒辛卯年刻竹紙 Cheng Yün Tzu Ti

Index Kuang Hsü Hsin Mao Nien Kò, Chu Chih
Dated, Kuang-Hsü "Hsin-Mao" 17/1891
Bamboo paper

Bound in 1 t'ao   10 Chuan   10 Tsé

Remarks

The University of Toronto Chinese Library

· ·

12

Accession No. 1311   Index No. 093— 2 cbk

Title 特別左傳 Tê Pieh Tso Chüan

Classification A 101

Subject a special expository notes on
左傳 Tso Chüan

References

Author Notes by 晉杜予頂   宋林堯叟 Chin, Tu—yu
Commentaries printed in red color   Sung, Ling Yao—Sou

Edition 細紅格板套印 Hsi Hung Ko Pan Tao Yin
中籍本精刊 Chin Hsiang Pên Ching K'an
Fine-printed, Pocket edition
石經山房藏本 "Mien hien" paper
                                    edition Pên
Index   Shih—Ching—shan—Fang Tsang Pên

Bound in   1 tao   50 chuan   16 tsê

Remarks

The University of Toronto Chinese Library

. . . .

117

Accession No.   1312   Index No. 038—市市 市市市

Title   姚端恪公文集 Yao Tuan Kö Kung Wên Chi

Classification   D

Subject

References

Author   清 姚文然 撰 Ching, Yao Wên-Jan Chuan

Edition   虚直軒藏版 Hsü-Chih-Hüan edition Tsang Pan

Bamboo paper. Chu Chih
竹紙

Index

Bound in   1 tao   19 Chuan   10 tse

Remarks

210

103

The University of Toronto Chinese Library

....

Accession No. *1314*   Index No. 0 ~~75~~ - *233 d*

Title   東里文集 *Tung Li Wên Chi*

Classification *D*

Subject

References

Author 清 楊士琦著 *Ching, Yang Shih-Chi Chu*

Edition 楊敦本堂藏版. *Yang-Tun-Pên Táng Tsáng Pan*

Index

Bound in *1 tao 25 chuan 6 tse*

Remarks

105

15

✓ ✓
Cab.I

Accession No. 1315   Index No. 067/zi

Title 文編

Classification not A, B C D 163 ⑤

Subject

References

Author 明唐順之選批 Ming, Tang Shun Chih

Edition 明嘉靖板   竹紙
                                    Bamboo paper
Date: Ming, Chia Ching

Index

Bound in 62 Chuan 30 tśe

Remarks

212

The University of Toronto Chinese Library

. . . .

102

Accession No. *1316*   Index No. *169 — Hfdf*

Title ~~D43~~ 關帝全書 *Kuan Ti Chüan Shu*

Classification ~~D43~~ C 368

Subject *A collection of Kwang's, the military saint, writing & biography with illustrated pictures.*

References

Author 清 黃啓曙彙輯 *Ching, Huang Chi-Shu Hui Chi*
                                      re-block-printing edition
Edition 王家瑞重列本 *Wang-Chia-Shui* ~~Chung Kan Pen~~
                                                      paper
         毛邊紙, 夾板 "*Moo-Pien*" ~~Chih~~, *Chia Pan*
                                              Wood-block

Index

Bound in   1 *tao*   40 *Chuan*   6 *tse*

Remarks

The University of Toronto Chinese Library

. . . .

57

Accession No. 1317   Index No. 039—mcld

Title 學仕遺規 Hsüeh shih I Kuei

Classification C

Subject

References

Author 清 陳宏謀 輯 Ch'ing, Chên Hung-Mou chi

Edition 福州正誼書院藏版 Fu-chou, Chêng-I Shu Yüan Ts'ang Pan (educational institute)

綿連紙 夾板 "Mien-Lien" Chih Chia Pan Wood-block (paper)

Index

Bound in   1 tao   4 chuan   10 ts'e

Remarks

214

The University of Toronto Chinese Library

· ·

24

Accession No.   1318   Index No. 096 — gmek

Title   理學宗傳 Li Hsüeh Tsung Chuan

Classification   B

Subject

References

Author   清 孫奇逢輯 Ching, Sun chi-Fêng chi

Edition   家藏版 ~~Chia Tsang Pon~~ Home Library
康熙年刻, 竹紙 ~~Kang Hsi Nien Kó~~, ~~Chu Chih~~
Dated, K'ang-Hsi period (1662-1722)
bamboo paper

Index

Bound in   1 tao,   26 chuan   8 tsê

Remarks

25

The University of Toronto Chinese Library

....

Accession No.   *1319*   Index No. *075—d9c9*

Title   東南紀事 *Tung Nan Chi shih*

Classification   *B 117   collected biographies.*

Subject   *A collection of the heroes of the later Ming Dynasty.*

References

Author   清 邵廷采 撰 *Ching, Shao Ting Tsai Chuan*

Edition   邵武徐氏校刊 *Shao-Wu, Hsü shih Chiao Kan*   *revised edition*

綿連紙   *"Mien-Lien" chih paper*

Index

Bound in   *1 Tao   12 Chuan   2 tsé*

Remarks

10

The University of Toronto Chinese Library

....

Accession No. 1320   Index No. 113—mc/g

Title 禮記鄭氏註 Li Chi Chêng shih chu

Classification A

Subject

References

Author 漢鄭康成註 Han, Chêng Kang-Chêng chu

Edition 味經書院刊 Wei-Ching educational institute chu yuan kan
光緒年刻 Kuang Hsü Nien K'o
白綿紙 夾板 "Pai-Mien" shih paper
Dated Kuang-Hsü period (1875-1908)

Index   Wood-block

Bound in   1 tao   20 chuan   10 tse

Remarks

The University of Toronto Chinese Library

. . . .

Accession No. ¹¹⁹ *1321*   Index No. *181 — cff*

Title 項城袁氏家集 *Hsiang Chʻêng Yüan Shih Chia Chi*

Classification D

Subject *a family collection of*

References

Author 清 袁甲三等撰 *Ching, Yüan Chia-San Têng Chuan and others*

Edition 清芬閣編刊本 *Ching-Fên-Ko Pien Kan Pên Block-printed edition*

宣統辛亥年刊 *Hsüan-Tung Hsin Hai Nien Kân*

洋紙 *"Yang" chih*

Index *Dated, Hsüan-Tung "Hsin-Hai" 3/1911*

Bound in *2 tao   56 tse*

Remarks

The University of Toronto Chinese Library

....

85

Accession No. *1322*   Index No. *163 — 3dd*

Title 邵子全集 *Shao Tzŭ Chüan Chi*

Classification C

Subject

References

Author 宋邵雍撰， 徐必達校正

Sung, Shao-Yung chuan, Hsü Pi-Ta ~~Chiao Cheng~~ *rivised*

Edition

竹紙，夾板 ~~Chu Chih~~, *Chia Pan Wood-block* *bamboo paper*

Index

Bound in 1 *tao* 24 *Chuan* 16 *tsê*

Remarks

The University of Toronto Chinese Library

. . . .

Accession No. *1323*   Index No. *031-bf6f*

Title 四書反身錄 *Szu Shu Fanshen Lu*

Classification *C*

Subject

References

Author 清李容著 *Ch'ing, Li Jung*

Edition 三韓劉氏版 *San Han Liu Shih*

Index

Bound in 八卷四冊 *8 Chüan, 4 Tsé*

Remarks 竹紙 *Bamboo Paper*

The University of Toronto Chinese Library

....

8

Accession No. *1324*   Index No. 032 — ~~item xi.~~ *l l cm*

Title 增廣字學舉隅 *Tsêng Kuang Tzǔ Hsüeh Chü Yü*

Classification A

Subject

References

Author 清 鐵 珊 輯 *Ching, Tieh-Shan Chi*

Edition 蘭州郡署刊版 *Lan-Chow Chün Kan Pan* *Block-printed*

同治甲戌年刊 綿連紙 *paper*
Tung Chih Chia shu Nien Kan "Mien-Lien" Chih

Index *Dated, Tung-Chih "Chia-Shu" 13/1874*

Bound in 1 *tao*   4 *tsê*

Remarks

The University of Toronto Chinese Library

．．．．．．．．．．．．．．．．．．．．．

84

Accession No. *1325*   Index No. *030*——錢

Title 唐一切經音義 *Táng I Ch'ieh Ching Ying I*

Classification   C

Subject

References

Author 清 莊炘等校正 *Ch'ing, Chuang Hsin* *Têng Chiao Chêng* *and others*

Edition 曹籀重刻 毛邊紙 夾版 *Ts'ao-Chou Chung Ke* *second edition* *"Mao-Pien" Chih, Chia Pan* *paper*

Index

Bound in 1 *tao*   25 *chuan*   4 *tse*

Remarks

The University of Toronto Chinese Library

. . . .

110

Accession No.   1326   Index No. 067 — 3/bi

Title   文章軌範 Wên Chang Kuei Fan

Classification   D

Subject

References

Author   宋 謝疊山 輯 Sung, Hsieh Tieh-Shan Chi

Edition   三韓劉氏藏版 San-Han, Liu Shih Tsʻang Pan
道光年刻 Tao-Kuang Nien Kʻo
竹 紙 Chu Chih

Index   Dated, Tao-Kuang period (1821—1850)
bamboo paper

Bound in   7 Chuan   1 Tsʻe

Remarks

223

The University of Toronto Chinese Library

. . . .

Accession No. *1327*   Index No. *009—人鏡類纂*

Title 人鏡類纂 *Jên Ching Lei Tsûan*

Classification C *13*   *Philosophy + related subjects*

Subject *A book on Chinese Virtues*

References

Author 清 程之禎 輯 *Ching, Ch'êng Chih—Chên Chi*

Edition 江夏 程氏藏 版 *Chiang-Hsia, Ch'êng Shih Ts'ang Pan*
黃毛太紙 *"Huang-Mao-T'ai" Chih paper*
同治癸酉年刻) *Tung-Chih Kuei-Yu Nien K'o*

Index *Dated, Tung-Chih "Kuei-Yu" 12/1893*

Bound in *2 Tao   46 chuan   16 ts'e*

Remarks

The University of Toronto Chinese Library

. . . .

28

Accession No.   1328   Index No. 146—3nkz/0足

Title   西藏圖考 Hsi Tsang Tu K'ao

Classification   B

Subject

References

Author   清. 黃沛翹 輯 Ching, Huang Pei-Chiao Chi

Edition   家藏版 Chia Tsang Pan Home Library

光緒丁酉年刻   毛邊紙 "Mao-Pien" paper

Kwang Hsü Ting Yu Nien Kõ

Mao Pien Chih

Index   Dated, Kwang-Hsü "Ting-Yu" 23/1897

Bound in   1 tao 4 tse (8 Chuan).

Remarks

225

The University of Toronto Chinese Library

. . . .

Accession No. 27 *1329*   Index No. *077—ĭebk*

Title 歷代史論 *Li Tai Shih Lun*

Classification *B*

Subject

References

Author ① 明 張溥 撰 　② 孫執升 評點 　① *Ming, Chang Tung Chon*
　　　　　　　　　　　　　　　　　② *Sun Chih-shêng Ping Tien*
Edition ③ 蒼松山房版 　③ *Tsang-Sung-Shan-Fong Pan edition*
　　④ 光緒年刻. 白紙 　④ *Kuang Hsü Nien Ko Pai Chih*
　　⑤ 硃版 夾版 　　⑤ *Red edition　　Wood-block*
Index 　　　　　　　　　 *Chu Pan,　Chia Pan*
　　　　　 ④ *Dated, Kuang-Hsü period (1875-1908) White paper*

Bound in 　1 tao　22 chuan　8 tsê.

Remarks

The University of Toronto Chinese Library
....

Accession No. 99 1330   Index No. 212 — 888⁴/4

Title 龍川文集 *Lung Chuan Wên Chi*

Classification D

Subject

References

Author 宋　陳亮撰 *Sung, Chên-Liang Chuan*

Edition 重刊本　退補齋藏版 *Second edition Chung Kan Pên Tui-Pu Chai tsang Pên edition*

Index

Bound in 1 *tao* 30 *chuan* 10 *tsê*

Remarks

The University of Toronto Chinese Library

. . . .

~~AB~~ 106

<u>Accession No.</u> *1331 A - B*   <u>Index No.</u> *037 — ~~a 131 力力力~~; 030 — ~~1321 力力~~*

<u>Title</u> 太樸生遺稿 一卷 *T'ai Pu Shêng I Kao   I Chüan*
古文摭遺 八卷 *Ku Wen Chih I   Pa Chüan*

<u>Classification</u> D 43   *Prose*

<u>Subject</u> *A- a collection y essays on historical personalities by Fu Yi chen q the Ching Synasty.*

B- a collection y famous essays by different writers

<u>References</u>

<u>Author</u> 清   傅以成著 *Ching, Chüan I-chêng Chu*

<u>Edition</u> 金礪堂藏版 *Chin-Li-Tang* ~~Tsang Pan~~ *edition*
同治年刻 *Dated, Tung-Chih Nien Kó period (1862-1874)*
竹紙 ~~Chu Chih~~ *bamboo paper*
夾版 ~~Chia Pan~~ *Wood-block*

<u>Index</u>

<u>Bound in</u> *1 tao* { *A - 1 Chuan   4 tsê*
                      B - 8 chuan   3 tsê

<u>Remarks</u>

The University of Toronto Chinese Library

....

Accession No. 69 _1332_   Index No. _128 — gilof_

Title 聖諭像解 _Shêng Yü Hsiang Chieh_

Classification _C_

Subject

References

Author 清 梁 延年 輯 _Ching, Liang Yen-Nien Chi_

Edition 廣州復初堂重刊, 古香閣藏版 _Kuang-Chow Fu-Chu_
綿連紙 _Têng Chung Kan, Ku-Hsiang-Ko Tsang Pan_ edited
Second edition
"Mien-Lien" Chih paper

Index

Bound in 1 tao 20 chuan 10 tsé

Remarks

The University of Toronto Chinese Library

....

Accession No. ~~92~~ *1333*   Index No. 075—*Li hò*

Title 樂道堂文鈔 *Lo Tạo Tảng Wên Chảo*

Classification   *D*

Subject

References

Author 清恭親王著 *Ching, Kung-Chin Wang* ~~Shu~~

Edition *Home Library* 家藏版 ~~*Chia Tsang Pan*~~
連史紙 夾版 "*Nien-Shih*" ~~*Chih*~~ ~~*Chia Pan*~~ *Wood-block*

Index

Bound in   1 tao   16 *Chuan*   16 *tsé.*

Remarks

The University of Toronto Chinese Library

....

Accession No. ^19 1334(A,B)   Index No.   012 — dhicht
                                            122 — dichh
                                            031 — hhichr

Title ① 明清題名碑錄 ②   A = 明題名碑錄
                        B = 圆朝題名石車錄

Classification B-117   ① Ming Ching Ti Ming Pei Lu

Subject   ② Ming Ti Ming Pei Lu

                       ③ Kuo Chao Ti Ming Pei Lu

References

Author 清國子監編 Ching, Kuo Tzu Chien Pien

Edition Official Edition 官版 Kuan Pan
        毛太紙　夾版 "Mao-Tai" Chih, Chia Pan Wood-block

Index

Bound in 2 tao(A,B) 14 chuan   14 Tsé

Remarks

The University of Toronto Chinese Library

. . . .

Accession No. 59 *1335*   Index No. *140—lhe*

Title 蕩寇志 *Tang Kou Chih*

Classification *C*

Subject

References

Author 清 俞仲華著 *Ching, Yü Chung-Hua Chu*

Edition 家藏版 *Chia Tsang Pan Home Library*

粉紙 *"Fèn" Chih paper*

Index

Bound in *2 tao 20 tse*

Remarks

The University of Toronto Chinese Library

·····················

Accession No. 93 *1336*   Index No. 060 — 9 ebed

Title 徐文定公集 *Hsü Wên Ting Kung Chi*

Classification *D*

Subject

References

Author 清李杕 輯 *Ching, Li-Ti Chi*

Edition 江南主教姚准刊 *Chiang-Nan, Chu Chiao Yao,*
油光紙 鉛印   *Chun-Kan*

                        "Yu-Kuang" paper Ch'ien Yin
Index   *Type-setting ed.*

Bound in 1 *tao*   6 *chuan*   4 *tsê*

Remarks

The University of Toronto Chinese Library

. . . .

Accession No. 70 1337   Index No. 102—98ᵉ

Title 畫家三昧 Hua Chia San Wei

Classification C

Subject

References

Author 清王竹禪繪 Ching, Wang Chu-Chan Hui

Edition 安禪堂刊 An-Chan-Tang Kan printed
綿連紙 夾版 "Mien-Nien" Chih paper Chia Pan Wood-block

Index

Bound in 1 tao   6 tsê

Remarks

2,   38

The University of Toronto Chinese Library
....

                    72
Accession No.   1338   Index No. 162—dek

Title   返性圖 Fan Hsing Tu

Classification   C 731

Subject

References

Author

Edition   思過齋藏版   SS-Ssu—Kuo Chih Chai Ts'ang Pan
                                              printed
           光緒三年重刊   白紙 Kuang Hsü Wu Nien Chung Kan
                                    Pai Chih
Index   Dated, Kuang—Hsü "Chi—Mao" 5/1879
                         White paper

Bound in   1 tao   10 Chuan   10 tsê

Remarks

                                              235

The University of Toronto Chinese Library
. . . .

113

Accession No. 1339   Index No. 067 Zeeh

Title 文苑英華辨證 Wên Yüan Ying Hua Pien Chêng

Classification D 93 Literary Critiques

Subject 10 volumes of literary criticism on the using
of words, names, places dates &c. by
Pan Hou Hsia of the Sung Dynasty reprinted
by the Royal Naval type of the Ching Court.

References

Author 宋 彭叔夏撰 Sung, Pêng Shu-Hsia Chuan

Edition 武英殿聚珍版 Wu-Ying-Tien Chü Chên Pan
Bamboo Paper Movable-type edition

Index

Bound in 1 Tao 4 tse

Remarks

236

The University of Toronto Chinese Library

. . . .

Accession No. 57 1340   Index No. 164 一gigg

Title 酉陽雜俎 Yu Yong Tsa Tsu

Classification C 328 Extracts from various works

Subject A collection of various topics compiled & edited ay by 段成式 of the Tang Dynasty.

References

Author 唐 段成式 撰 Tang, Tuan Hsia Ch'eng-Shih Chuan

Edition 崇文書局 版 Chung-Wen Shu Chü Pan Book Co. edition
光緒三年刻, 粉織 夾板
Kuang Hsü San Nien K'o
"Fen" Chih paper Chia Pan Wood-block

Index Dated, Kuang-Hsü "Ting-Chou" 3/1877

Bound in 1 tao   20 chuan   6 tse.

Remarks

237

The University of Toronto Chinese Library

. . . .

58 ˅

Accession No. 1341   Index No. 001— d 9919

Title 世説新語 Shih Shuo Hsing Yü

Classification C 368 Colloquial Novels.

Subject Short stories on historical personalities with special bearing on moral exhortation.

References

Author 宋劉義慶撰 Sung, Liu I-Ching Chuan

Edition 崇文書局列, Chung-Wen Shu Chü Kan Book co; edition
光緒三年刻 粉紙 英版
Kuang Hsü San Nien K'o
"Fên" Chih paper Chia Pan Wood-block

Index Dated, Kuang-Hsü "Ting Chou" 3/1877

Bound in 1 tao   6 chuan   4 tse

Remarks

238

The University of Toronto Chinese Library
....

57

Accession No.　1342　　　　Index No. 085 — 9ₙ³C鈞k

Title　涷水紀聞 *Su Shui Chi Wên*

Classification ² C 308

Subject　"*A historical account of the Sung Dynasty by* 司馬光 *Ssŭ Ma Kuang*

References

Author　宋司馬光撰 *Sung, Ssŭ-Ma-Kuang Chuan*

Edition　崇文書局刋 *Chung-Wen Shu Chü Kan* Book Co. edition
　　　　光緒三年刻 *Kuang Hsü San Nien K'o*
　　　　粉紙　夾板 "*Fên" Chih　Chia Pan* Wood-block

Index　　*Dated, Kuang-Hsü "Ting-Chou" 3/1877*

Bound in　1 tao　16 chuan　4 tsé

Remarks

The University of Toronto Chinese Library

....

119

Accession No. *1343*   Index No. *120—lbca*

Title 繡虎軒尺牘 *Hsiu Hu Hsien Chih Tu*

Classification *D*

Subject

References

Author 清 曹煜著 *Ching, Tsao-Yü Chu*

Edition 傳萬堂梓行 *Chuan-Wan-Tang Tzu Hsing*
毛邊紙 *"Mao-Pien" Chih paper*

Index

Bound in 3 tao 24 chuan 24 tsé

Remarks

The University of Toronto Chinese Library

. . . .

98

Accession No. *1344*　　　　Index No. *118 — edken*

Title 笠翁傳奇十種 *Li Wêng Ch'üan Chi Shih Chung*

Classification *D 147*

Subject *10* ~~book~~ *Romances of ballads type by Li Yu of the Ching Dynasty*

References

Author 清李漁撰 *Ching, Li-Yü Chuan*

Edition 世德堂藏版 *Shih-Tê-Táng Tsáng Pan*
毛邊紙 *"Mao-Pien" Chih paper*
夾版 *Chia Pan Wood-block*

Index

Bound in *2 tao　20 tsê*

Remarks

The University of Toronto Chinese Library

. . . .

72

Accession No.　　1345　　　Index No. 140—巭ie

Title　蘇黃題跋 *Su Huang T'i Po*
　　　　　　附尺牘小詞 *Fu Chih Tu Hsiao Tz'u*

Classification　　C

Subject

References

Author　明黃嘉惠校 *Ming, Huang Chia-Hui Chiao*

Edition　明刻本　　*Ming, K'ên Pên*
　　　竹紙 夾曲版 *Chu Chih Chia Pan*
　　　　　　bamboo paper Wood-block

Index　　　　*Dated, Ming Dynastie (1368-1643)*

Bound in　1 t'ao　16 chuan　8 tse

Remarks

46

The University of Toronto Chinese Library

....

Accession No. 79 / 1346   Index No. 031 — dm cfh

Title 困學紀聞 *Kún Hsüeh Chi Wên*

Classification C - 308

Subject

References *Toronto No. 910*

Author 宋 王應麟 撰 *Sung, Wang Ying-Lin Chuan*

Edition 清河義門 校本 *Ching-Ho I-Mên Chiao Pên (Rivised edition)*
桐華書塾刻 *Tung-Hua-Shu-Shu printed*
毛邊紙 *"Mao-Pien" Chih paper*

Index

Bound in 1 *tao* 20 *chuan* 6 *tse.*

Remarks

47

The University of Toronto Chinese Library

....

Accession No. 1347   Index No. 173—if i C

Title 霞客遊記 Hsia Kó Yu Chi

Classification B . 222

Subject

References

Author 明. 徐宏祖著 Ming, Hsü Hung-Tsu Chu

Edition 水心齋葉氏刻本 Shui-Hsin-Chai, Yeh Shih Kó Pen, printed
毛邊紙 "Mao-Pien" Chih paper
嘉慶戊辰校補本 Chia-Ching "Hsü-Chên" Chiao Rivised Re-Pu Pen, printed

Index

Bound in 2 tao   10 tse

Remarks

The University of Toronto Chinese Library

. . . .

31

Accession No.   1348   Index No. 120 — 亦有另法

Title 約章成案滙覽 *Yüeh* Chang Ch'eng An Hui Lan

Classification B

Subject

References

Author [1]北洋洋務局纂輯 [1]*Pei Yang, Yang Wu Chü Tsuan chi*

Edition [2]上海點石齋印   [3]洋粉連紙
   [4]夾板   [2] *Shang-Hai, Tien-Shih-Chai Ying* printed
   [3] *"Yang-Fēn-Nien" Chih paper*

Index   [4] *Chia Pan Wood-block*

Bound in   2 tao   Part I 10 Chuan 10 tae
Remarks   Part II 42 "   42 "

245

The University of Toronto Chinese Library

. . . .

49

Accession No. *1349*   Index No. *053—lj dc*

Title 廣博物志 *Kuang Po Wu Chih*

Classification *C*

Subject

References

Author 清董斯張著 *Ching, Tung Ssŭ-Chang Chu*

Edition 高輝堂藏版 *Kao-Hui-Tang Tsang Pan edition*

乾隆辛巳年刻 *Ch'ien Lung Hsin Ssŭ Nien K'o*

毛邊紙 *"Mao-Pien" Chih paper*

Index *Dated, Ch'ien-Lung "Hsin-Ssŭ" 26/1761*

Bound in *8 Tao 40 tsé (50 Chuan)*

Remarks

The University of Toronto Chinese Library
....

Accession No. 1350   Index No. 010—6

21

Title 元西域人華化考 (稿本) Yüan Hsi Yü jén Hua Hua Kăo (Kăo Pén)

Classification β

Subject

References

Author 陳垣 撰 Ch'ên —Yüan Chuan

Edition 謄寫版印本 Téng Hsieh Pan Ying Pên
Manuscript Block-printing edition

毛邊紙 夾版 "Mao-Pien" Chih Chia Pan
paper wood-block

Index

Bound in 1 tao 2 tsê

Remarks

The University of Toronto Chinese Library

. . . .

107

Accession No. *1351*   Index No. *072 — dhe d*

Title   明朝破邪集 *Ming Chao Po Hsieh Chi*

Classification *D-985*

Subject

References

Author   明, 徐昌治 訂 *Ming, Hsü Chʻang-Chih Ting*

Edition   日本安政乙卯年翻刻本 *Jih-Pên, An-Chêng "I Mao" Nien*
高麗紙   *Fan Kʻo Pên*
translated edition

          "Kao-Li" Chih paper

Index

Bound in   *8 chuan   8 tsê*

Remarks

52

. . . .

Accession No.   '7   1352   Index No. 025 — bep dicti

Title   朱伯廬先生編年毋欺錄

Classification   B Chu Po Lu Hsien Shêng pien Nien Wu Chi Lu

Subject

References

Author   金吳瀾編   Chin Wu-Lan Pien

Edition   家藏版   Chia Ts'ang Pan Home Library

Index

Bound in   1 Tao   3 Chuan   6 Tsê

Remarks

249

. . . .

Accession No.   HO 13 53   Index No. 037—a h f b 套

Title   天祿閣外史 Tien Lu Ko Wai Shih

Classification   B-52 雜史

Subject

References

Author   明鄺黃愚著 Ming, Kuang-Yü Chü

Edition   明嘉靖版 Ming Chia Ching Pan
          竹紙   Chu Chih bamboo paper
                   Dated, Ming "Chia-Ching" edition

Index

Bound in   8 tao   2 tse

Remarks

250

The University of Toronto Chinese Library
. . . .
103

Accession No.   1354   Index No. 173-C lff 封面

Title   雪橋詩話三集 Hsüeh Chiao Shih Hua San Chi

Classification   D 93   Literary Critiques

Subject   a collection of life + interesting
accounts of some chinese poems
+ poets.

References

Author   清 楊 鍾義 選集 Ching, Yang. Chung-I Hsüan Chi

Edition   求恕齋刊   竹紙   夾版
            Chiu-Shu-Chai Ko   edition bamboo paper Wood-block
            Chu Chih Chia Pan

Index

Bound in   2 tao   12 chuan   20 tse

Remarks

The University of Toronto Chinese Library

. . . .

Accession No.   *111*   1355   Index No. ~~140~~ *201 -3d16d* ~~d16d~~

Title   黄忠端公集   *Huang Chung Tuan Kuang Chi*

Classification   D

Subject

References

Author   明 黄尊素著 *Ming, Huang Tsun-Su Chu*

Edition   正氣堂刊   姚江黄氏藏版

Chêng-Chi-Tâng Kʻo edition

Index   *Yao-Chiang, Huang Shih Tsang Pan* *edition*

Bound in   1 tao 6 chuan   3 tsê.

Remarks

The University of Toronto Chinese Library

. . . .

103

Accession No.   1356   Index No. 075－d̷ᵉ₁d

Title   東里別集 Tung Li Pieh Chi

Classification   D

Subject

References

Author   清   楊士琦輯錄 Ching, Yang Shih-Chi
                                                    Chi Lu

Edition   家藏版 Chia Tsàng Pan Home Library
          毛邊紙 "Mao-Pien" Chih paper
          夾版   Chia Pan Wood-block

Index

Bound in   1 tao   4 tsè

Remarks

68

Accession No. *1357*   Index No. *057 —— diz*

Title 弟子箴言 *Ti Tzŭ Chên Yen*

Classification *C*

Subject

References

Author 清 胡達源 撰 *Chíng, Hu Ta-yuan Chuan*

Edition 蒲圻 但氏 刊本 *Pu-Chí, Tan-Shih Kân Pên*

光緒 乙未年 刊 *Kwang Hsü I Wei Nien Kân*

毛邊紙 *"Mao-Pien" Chih paper*

Index *Dated, Kuang-Hsü "I-Wei" 21/1895*

Bound in 16 *Chuan* 4 *Tsé*

Remarks

The University of Toronto Chinese Library

· ·

33

Accession No.   1358   Index No. 046—efknl

Title   岣嶁墬鑑樣 Kou Lou Chien Ts'o

Classification β32 complete historical narrative

Subject a summary of Chinese ~~primitive~~
history. from the begining to the
ming Dynasty. with chronology.

References

Author 清 曠 敏本篆 Ching, Kuang Min Pên Tsuan

Edition 家藏版 Chia Tsàng Pan Home library
嘉慶年刻 楊霈藏 白竹紙夾版
                          period (1796-1820)
Dated, Chia-Ching Nien Ko   Yàng-Péi Tsàng
                      Pai Chu Chih   Chia Pan
                  White bamboo paper Wood-block

Index

Bound in 1 tao   4 chuan   4 Tse.

Remarks

The University of Toronto Chinese Library
. . . .

46

Accession No. *1359*　　　　Index No. *010 — d9ph*

Title 先哲叢談 *Hsien Chê Ts'ung Tân*

Classification *B 117 Collected biographies*

Subject *a collection of Japanese literary scholars' biographies with chronology + note. Published in Japan.*

References

Author 日本 東條耕子藏著 *(Jih-Pên) Tung-T'sao Kêng-Tzǔ Tsǎng Chu*

Japan

Edition 日本版, 日本皮紙 *Japanese version*

Jih Pên Pǎn, Jih Pên P'i Chih Japanese Leather paper

Index

Bound in 　　　　8 *Chuan* 10 *tsé*

Remarks

The University of Toronto Chinese Library

. . . .

62

Accession No. 1360   Index No. 030—bf3

Title   古格言 *Ku Ko Yen*

Classification   C 328   Extracts from various works
compiled & edited

Subject   a collection of famous sayings
under 12 main topics.

References

Author   清 梁章鉅 輯 *Ching, Liang Chang Chü Chi*

Edition   任位俊籌重刊 *Jên-Wei-Chün Teng Chung Kan*
and others Second edition

毛邊紙   "*Mao-Pien*" Chih paper

Index

Bound in   1 *tao*   12 *chuan*   4 *tsé*

Remarks

The University of Toronto Chinese Library
. . . .

40

Accession No.   *1361*   Index No. *140—hcec*

Title   莱州府志 *Lai Chow Fu Chih*

Classification   *B*

Subject

References

Author   清 嚴有禧纂修 *Ching, Yen Yu-Hsi Tsuan Hsiu*

Edition   官版   *Kuan Pan official copy*

乾隆年刻 白紙 *Dated: Chien-Lung Nien Kó Pai Chih*
period (1036-1095)
White paper

Index

Bound in   *1 tao   16 chuan   8 tśe*

Remarks

62

The University of Toronto Chinese Library
. . . .

60

Accession No.   1362   Index No. 162—ec

Title   述 記   Shu Chih Chi

Classification   C 328 Extracts from various worked.

Subject   A summary of important extracts
from different historical & philosophical
book preparing for beginners.

References

Author   清 任文田 撰   Ch'ing, Jen Wen Tien Chuan

Edition   映雪草堂藏版   Ying-Hsüeh-Ts'ao-T'ang Ts'ong Pan
毛邊紙   "Mao-Pien" Chih paper

Index

Bound in   1 Tao   4 t'se

Remarks

259

The University of Toronto Chinese Library

. . . .

49

Accession No. _1363_   Index No. 085—哲子

Title   汪子中詮 Wang Tzǔ Chung Chüan

Classification   C—13 哲学

Subject

References

Author 明 汪應蛟撰 Ming, Wang Ying-Chiao Chuan

Edition 明萬曆刊本   Ming Wan Li Kʻan Pên
        白紙 夾版   Pai Chih Chia Pan Wood-block
                     White paper

Index

Bound in   1 tao   6 chuan   6 tse

Remarks

64

. . . .

98

Accession No.   1364   Index No. 025-Wil

Title   楚辭 Chʻu Tzʻŭ

Classification   D

Subject

References

Author   漢 劉 向 集 Han, Liu Hsiang Chi

Edition   大字版   Ta Tzŭ Pan
          綿連紙 夾板 "Mien-Lien" Chih Chia Pan   paper Wood-block

Index

Bound in   1 Tao   17 chuan   4 tse

Remarks

261

The University of Toronto Chinese Library

. . . .

59   see also 1384 same book

Accession No.   1365   Index No. 140 — 廖氏九

Title   蔡氏九儒書 Ts'ai Shih Chiu-Ju Shu
              附蔡氏通譜 福州外紀

Classification   C-13 Fu Ts'ai Shih Tung P'u   Fu Chow Wai Chi

Subject a collection of the history, works, scholars
of the Tsai family.

References

Author   清 蔡發撰 Ch'ing, Ts'ai-Fa Chuan

Edition 三餘書屋藏版 San-Yu-Shu-Wu Tsang Pan
              同治戊辰春刻 Tung Chih Hsü Chên Chun K'o
              綿連紙   "Mien-Lien" chih paper
Index   Dated, Tung-Chih "Hsü-Chên 7/1868

Bound in   1 tao 8 chuan 6 tsé
                  and 10 chuan 1 tsé
Remarks   another 1 chuan 1 tsé

The University of Toronto Chinese Library

. . . .

85

Accession No.   1366   Index No. 015-kgg9.

Title   净土津梁 Ching T'u Ching Liang

Classification   C -

Subject

References

Author   Buddhist monk   了 慰 Liao-Wei
                                        period (1734-1820)
Edition   乾隆年刻 竹纸 Chien-Lung Hien-Ko
                              Chu Chih
                                  bamboo paper

Index

Bound in   1 tao   15 chuan 9 tse.

Remarks

The University of Toronto Chinese Library

. . . .

26

Accession No. *1367*   Index No. *030—6P*

Title   史 懷 *Shih Huai*

Classification *B – 137   Historical Excerpts.*

Subject *A historical & literary discussion on Chinese personalities from different books.*

References

Author 明 鍾 惺 輯 *Ming, Chung-Hsing Chi*

Edition 餘草堂藏版 *Yu-Tsao-Tang Tsang Pan*
光緒辛卯年刻 *Kuang-Hsü "Hsin-Mao" Nien K'o* Dated: 17/1891.
(*Bamboo paper*) *Chu Chih.*

Index   竹 紙

Bound in   *1 tao   20 Chuan   6 tsê*

Remarks

68

✓

Cab. I

The University of Toronto Chinese Library
. . . .
18

Accession No.   1368   Index No. 050—fnkg

Title   帝鑑圖說 *Ti Chien Tu Shuo*

Classification   B 137   Historical Excerpts.

Subject   A collection of moral and just administration of the past Emperors. The book prepared for the teaching of young princes.

References

Author   明 張居正著 *Ming, Chang Chü-Chêng Chu*

Edition   江陵鄧氏藏版 *Chiang-Ling, Têng-Shih Tsang Pan*
白綿紙   "*Pai-Mien*" *Chih paper*

Index

Bound in   1 tao   4 Chuan   4 tsé.

Remarks

265

The University of Toronto Chinese Library

. . . .

85

Accession No.   1369   Index No. 037--eah

Title   奉天錄 Fêng Tien Lu

Classification   C 33 Military affairs

Subject   A record of the military operation
at Feng Tien.

References

Author   唐 趙元一撰 Táng, Chao Yüan-1 Chuan

Edition   亨掃精舍刊 Hêng-Sao-Ching-Shê Kára
道光年刻 綿紙 Tao Kuang Nien KO "Mien" Chih paper
夷山王氏藏 I-Shan, Wang-Shih Tsàng

Index   Dated, Tao-Kuang period (1821-1850)

Bound in   1 tao   4 Chuan   2 tsê

Remarks

266

The University of Toronto Chinese Library
. . . .

64

Accession No. 1370   Index No. 024 — 33c3 Efgb

Title 十竹齋書畫譜 Shih Chu Chai Shu Hua Pu

Classification   C

Subject

References   Hu Yüeh-Ts'ang Mu Ku

Author 明 胡曰從摹古 Ming, Hu Yüeh Chung

Edition 張學畊重刊 Chang-Hsüeh-Kêng Chung Kon
       綿連紙 "Mien-Lien" Chih paper

Index

Bound in 1 Tao 8 tse.

Remarks

267

The University of Toronto Chinese Library

. . . .

108

Accession No. *1371*　　　　Index No. ~~A53~~ *030—gfba*

Title　唐詩三百首補註

Classification　*D*　*Tang Shih San Pai Shou Pu Chu*

Subject

References

Author　清 女史　陳伯英輯　*Ch'ing, Nü-shih*
　　　　　　　　　　　　　　Ch'ên Po-ying Chi

Edition　四藤吟社刊　*Ssu-T'eng-Yin-Shê Kan*

Index

Bound in　*1 tao　8 chuan　4 ts'e*

Remarks

72

✓
✓
Cab. I

The University of Toronto Chinese Library

. . . .

86

Accession No. 1372   Index No. 036 — 夢溪筆談

Title 夢溪筆談 Mêng Chi Pi Tan

Classification C 306

Subject A collection of miscellaneous essays, Stra stories, discussion by Shen Tien of the Sung Dynasty.

References

Author 宋沈适著 Sung, Shên-Kua Chu

Edition 明刻本 Ming, Ko Pên Dynastie (1368-1643)
竹紙 Chu Chih bamboo paper

Index

Bound in 1 tao 26 chuan 8 tse

Remarks

269

73

The University of Toronto Chinese Library
....
58

Accession No.   1373   Index No. 001—2gig

Title   世說新語 Shih Shuo Hsing Yu

Classification C - 368 Miscellaneous narratives & records.

Subject A collection of interesting accounts of
historical characters with bearing &
exhortation on certain virtues.

References

Author 宋劉義慶撰 Sung, Liu I-Ching Chuan

Edition 粉紛坎閣版 Fên-Hsing-Ko Pan
白紙 Pai Chih White paper

Index

Bound in 1 tao 6 chuan 6 tse

Remarks

270

The University of Toronto Chinese Library

. . . .

Accession No.   127
                 1374   Index No. 001-3c/Pf

Title   一齋叢書 I Chai Ts'ung Shu

Classification   C-338
                  why c not 2

Subject

References

Author   清 郝一齋著 Ching, Hao I-Chai Chu

Edition 王容若校刊 Wang-Jung-Jo Chiao Kan Revised edition
         共四種, 毛邊紙 Kung Ssu Chung, "Mao-Pien" paper Chih
                      Four kinds

Index

Bound in   1 tao 5 chuan 4 ts'e.

Remarks

The University of Toronto Chinese Library

. . . .

Accession No. 93 1375   Index No. 102—ah jáz

Title 申椒園 二集 Shên Chiao Yuan Erh Chi

Classification D

Subject

References

Author 清 黃勷著 Ching, Huang-Jang Chu

Edition 醉山樓版 Tsui-Shan-Lou Pan

嘉慶 壬戌年刻 Chia Ching Jên ⊕ Hsü Nien K'o

Index 貴州 棉紙 Kuen-Chow, "Mien" Chik chih paper

Dated, Chia-Ching "Jên-Hsü" 7/1802

Bound in   1 tao   2 chuan   3 tse.

Remarks

The University of Toronto Chinese Library

....

Accession No. 9 1376   Index No. 149—hgfe

Title 論語解註合編 Lun Yü Chieh Chu Ho Pien

Classification A

Subject

References

Author 清 姚永樸 註 Ch'ing, Yao Yung-Pu Chu

Edition 秋浦翰墨林 石印 (Lithographic Version)
毛邊紙 Chiu-Pu-Han-Mo-Ling Shih Ying
"Mao-Pien" Chih paper

Index

Bound in 1 tao 10 chuan 2 tse.

Remarks

The University of Toronto Chinese Library

. . . .

Accession No.   9 1377   Index No. 149—fb99&9

Title   詩三家義集疏 Shih San Chia I Chi Su

Classification   A

Subject

References

Author   清王先謙著 Ching, Wang Hsien-Chien Chu

Edition   虛受堂刊本 Hsü-Shou-Tang Kan Pen

毛邊紙   "Mao-Pien" Chih paper

Index

Bound in   1 tao   28 chuan   10 tsé.

Remarks

274

The University of Toronto Chinese Library

. . . .

50

Accession No.   *1378*   Index No. *125—老 ZZC*

Title   老子衍 *Lao Tzŭ Yen*

Classification   *C 731. Taoism.*

Subject   *An exposition of Laotze's book.*

References

Author   李惺樵 *Li 懼 Hsing-Ch'iao*

Edition   *(Home Edition)* 家藏板 *Chia Tsang Pan*
自然室雜述之一 *Tzŭ-Jan-Shih Tsa Shu Chih 1*
綿連紙 *"Mien-Lien" Paper*

Index

Bound in   *1 tsê.*

Remarks

The University of Toronto Chinese Library
. . . .

32

Accession No.   1379   Index No. 180—16

Title   韻夂史 Yün Shih

Classification B 52 Miscellaneous historical writing

Subject A book of historical essays as in metrical form, covering from the primitive time down to the Ming Dynasty.

References

Author 清許邂菴編 Ching, Hsü Tün-An

Edition 十年讀書之廬重刊 Shih-Nien-Tu-shu-Chih-Lu Chang Kan _Second edition_
咸豐年刻 綿連紙 Dated, Hsien-Fêng period (1851-1861)

Index   "Mien-Lien" paper

Bound in   1 tao   2 chuan   1 tsê.

Remarks

276

The University of Toronto Chinese Library

. . . .

3

Accession No. *1380*   Index No. *095 —* ~~m888~~ ~~mfg...888~~

Title 檀弓考工 二通 *Tan Kung Kǎo Kung Ērh Tung*

Classification *A 71 Ritualistic literature*

Subject *a book on ritualistism, mainly with funerals, illustrated with historical + literary references.*

References

Author 清 徐穆如 輯註 *Ching, Hsü Mu-ju*

Edition *Home Library* 家藏版
篤素堂張曉漢藏 *Tu-Su T'ang, Chang Shi Hsiao-Yu T'ang*
竹紙 *Bamboo paper*

Index

Bound in *1 tao   8 chuan   8 tsé.*

Remarks

277

?   81

The University of Toronto Chinese Library
. . . .

28

Accession No.   1381   Index No. 128—米f

Title   聖廟祀典圖考 Shêng Miao Ssŭ Tien Tú Kao

Classification   B-117 傳記-總錄

Subject — Biographies of <u>Confucius</u> and his disciples
and followers; with illustrations; places occupied
in the confucian Temple; and eulogies of
various emperors.

References

Author   清 顧沅 輯 Ch'ing, Ku-Yüan
                                    Private-printed edition
Edition   賜硯堂家藏版 Tzŭ-Kuan-Tang, Chia Tsang Pan

           道光年刻 Dated, Tao-Kuang period (1821-1850)
           粉紙   "Fen" paper

Index

Bound in   1 tao   5 Chuan   6 tsê.

Remarks

278

61

The University of Toronto Chinese Library

....

Accession No. *1382*　　　Index No. *077/nbk*

Title 歸元鏡 *Kuei Yuan Ching*

Classification 芥子園畫傳

Subject

References

Author 釋智達拈頌 *Shih Chih Ta*

Edition 乾隆甲辰年刊本　　　綿連紙

Dated: Chien Lu Chia Chen Nien　　*"Mien-lien" paper*

Index *ch'ing, Chia-ching period 23rd year*

Bound in 二 *Chüan* 之 *tsa*

Remarks 4 *tsè*

279

The University of Toronto Chinese Library

. . . .

61

Accession No.   1383   Index No. 077—Nhk

Title   歸元鏡 Kuei Yüen Ching

Classification   C

Subject

References

Author   釋　智達拈頌 Shih Chih—Ta

Edition   乾隆甲甲辰年刊本 Dated, Chien-Lung "Chia-Chen".
          綿連紙 "Mien Lien" paper   49/1784

Index

Bound in 1 tao   2 chuan   2 t'se.

Remarks

The University of Toronto Chinese Library

· ·

Accession No. 1383 / 1384   Index No. 077-nbk

Title 歸元鏡 Kuei Yüan Ching

Classification C—513 釋氏

Subject Buddhism ; with pictures

References

Author 釋智達批纂 Shih Chih-Ta

Edition 乾隆甲辰年刊于, 綿連紙
Dated Chien-Lung "Chia Chên"/ 1784
"Mien-Lien" paper

Index a general table of contents for 2 chüan

Bound in 1 t'ao, 2 chüan, 2 ts'ê

Remarks

The University of Toronto Chinese Library

. . . .

Accession No. 59 1384   see also 1365

Index No. 140-kgan

Title 蔡氏九儒書 *Ts'ai Shih Chiu Ju Shu*

Classification C 13 Philosophy & related subjects.

Subject a collection of various history of school & scholars of the Tsai family

References

Author 清 蔡發撰 *Ching, Ts'ai-Fa*

Edition 三餘書屋藏版 *San-Gu-Shu-Wu Ts'ong Pan*
同治戊辰春鐫 *Dated, Tung-Chih "Wu-Chên" 7/1868*
綿連紙 *"Mien-Lien" paper*

Index

Bound in 1 Tao 8 Chuan 6 Tsê

Remarks

The University of Toronto Chinese Library

. . . .

Accession No. *1385*   Index No. *168 — gihm*

Title 同治十年

長編總檔 *Ch'ang Pien Chung Tsung Tang*

Classification *B-67*

Subject

References

Author

Edition 寫本 *Hsieh Pen Manuscript copy, print in red*
東昌綿紙 硃格 *"Tung-Ch'ang-Mien" paper*
清同治十年 *Ch'ing, Tung-Chih "Hsing-Wei" 10/1871*

Index

Bound in   1 *tao*   12 *Chuan*   12 *tsé*

Remarks

XR.B.

87

√ √
Cab. I

The University of Toronto Chinese Library

. . . .

20

Accession No. *1386*   Index No. *168 — gikm*

Title 同治十一年 長編總檔 *Chang Pien Tsung Tang*

Classification ß-67

Subject

References

Author

Edition 寫本   東昌錦紙   *Manuscript Copy* *print in red* *Hsieh Pen, "Tung Chang Mien" paper*
         硃格   清同治十一年   *Dated, Ching, Tung-Chih "Jen-Shen" 11/1872*

Index

Bound in 1 tao   12 chuan   12 tśe

Remarks

284

8

Accession No.   1387   Index No. 149—89

Title   詩經 Shih Ching

Classification   A

Subject

References

Author   明 鍾惺 批點 Ming, Chung-Hsing

Edition   明凌杜若自刊本   硃批評選
Ming Ling Tu-Jo Kan Pên   Chu Pi Ping Hsüan
棉連紙 "Mien-Lien" paper

Index

Bound in   1 tao   6 tsé.

Remarks

285

The University of Toronto Chinese Library
. . . .

127

Accession No. _1388_   Index No. _10年一九四九_

Title   當歸草堂叢書 _Tāng Kuei Tsʼáo Tang Chung Shu_

Classification   C - 338

Subject

References

Author   人

Edition   錢唐丁氏重刊本 _Chien-Tāng, Ting Shih Chung Kan Pēn_
           同治二年刊 _Dated, Tung-Chih "Kuei-Hai" 2/1863_
           毛邊紙 _"Mao-Pien" paper_

Index

Bound in   1 tao   8 tse

Remarks

The University of Toronto Chinese Library

. . . .

103

Accession No. *1389*　　　　Index No. ~~440~~
　　　　　　　　　　　　　　　　　006—khhf

Title　慕萊堂詩文徵存 *Mu Lai Tang Shih Wên Chêng Tsún*

Classification　*D33　Verse & Prose*

Subject　*a collection of verse & prose.*

References

Author　清 李維翰 編 *Ching　Li Wei-Han*

Edition　家藏版 *Chia Tsáng Pan Home library
(Home Edition)*

Index

Bound in　*1 Tao　10 Chuan　4 tsé*

Remarks

The University of Toronto Chinese Library

. . . .

74

Accession No. *1390*   Index No. *032—1gd*

Title 墨子閒話 *Mo Tzŭ Hsien Ku*

Classification *C*

Subject

References

Author 清 孫詒讓 撰 *Ching, Sun I-jang*

Edition 家藏版 *Chia Tsang-Pan (Home edition)*

光緒年刻 *Dated, Kuang-Hsü period (1825—1908)*

連史紙 *"Lien-Shih" paper*

Index

Bound in   1 tao   15 chuan   8 tse.

Remarks

√

The University of Toronto Chinese Library

. . . .

55

Accession No. *1391*   Index No. ~~C67~~
                                        076—*he 27*

Title 欽定各郊壇廟樂章
       Ch'in Ting ~~Ko~~ *Chiao T'an Miao* ~~Ko~~ *Chang*   Ko.   yüeh

Classification C

Subject

References

Author 清 張樂盛彙輯 *Ching, Chang Lo-shêng*

Edition 神樂署重刻 *Shên-Ko-Shu Chung Ko*
         道光年刻 *Dated, Tao-Kuang period (1821—1850)*
         竹紙   *bamboo paper*

Index

Bound in   1 *tao*   2 *tsê.*

Remarks

The University of Toronto Chinese Library
. . . .

60

Accession No. *1392*   Index No. *147—pqgh*

n.d

Title 觀世音菩薩大悲陀羅尼經咒

Classification C *Kuan shih ying Pu Sa Ta Pei To Lo Ni Ching Chou*

Subject

References

Author 伽梵達摩譯 *Chia Fan Ta Mo*

Edition 咸豐元年刻 *Dated, Hsien—Fêng "Hsing-Hai" 1/1851*
白紙   *White paper*

Index

Bound in | *tao* | *tse*

Remarks

290

The University of Toronto Chinese Library

. . . .

72

Accession No.　　1393　　　　Index No. 009—eef $\overset{a}{x}$

Title　佛祖統系道影 Fo Tsu Tung Hsi Tao Ying

Classification　C

Subject

References

Author　釋守一重刻本 Shih, Shou-1

Edition　綿連紙　"Mien-Lien" paper

Index

Bound in　1 Tao　4 Chuan　4 Tse.

Remarks

. . . .

63

Accession No.   1394   Index No. 053-948

Title   庭訓格言 Ting Hsün Ko Yen

Classification   C-13

Subject

References

Author   清聖祖皇帝製 Ch'ing, Shêng-Tsu Hung Ti (Emperor)

Edition   殿版 Tien Pan Palace edition
          綿連紙 "Mien-Lien" paper

Index

Bound in   1 tsê.

Remarks

292

96

The University of Toronto Chinese Library
. . . .

Accession No. 1395   Index No. 007-69

Title   五經 Wu Ching

Classification   A

Subject

References

Author

Edition 江南書局刻本 Chiang Nan Shu Chü Kó Pen Book Co.
         綿連紙   "Mien-Lien" paper

Index

Bound in   6 tao   29 tse.

Remarks

293

✓ 97

✓
Cab I

110

Accession No.   1396   Index No. 140-kidd

Title   蔣道林先生文粹

Classification   D Chiang Tao Ling Hsien Shêng Wên Sui

Subject

References

Author   明 姚世英等銓次 Ming, Yao Shih-Ying and others

Edition   明萬曆版 Ming, Wan-Li period (1573—1620)

Index

Bound in   1 tao   13 chuan   5 tse.

Remarks

294

. . . .

7 98

Accession No. 9 1397   Index No. 082-88fd

Title 毛詩品物圖考 Mao Shih Pin Wu Tu Kǎo

Classification A 31

Subject

References

Author 浪華岡元鳳纂輯 Lang-Hua Kang-Yüan-Fêng

Edition 日本版 Japanese edition

高麗綿紙 Korea "Mien" paper

Index

Bound in 1 tao 7 chuan 4 tśe.

Remarks

The University of Toronto Chinese Library

. . . .

103

Accession No. *1398*   Index No. *061-g3d*

Title 悦心集 *Yüeh Hsin Chi*

Classification *D 63 general collection of verse &*

Subject *a general collection of verse & Prose*
prose mainly on natural appreciation
& ascetic tendency.

References

Author 清雍正帝御選 *Ch'ing, Yung-Chêng*
(Emperor)

Edition 聚珍版 *Chü Chên Pan Movable-type edition*
綿連紙 *"Mien-Lien" paper*

Index

Bound in *1 tao   4 chuan   2 tsé.*

Remarks

100

The University of Toronto Chinese Library
....

Accession No. 71 1399   Index No. 042—eci
                                        042—eqi
Title 尚直編 Shang Chih Pien
       尚理編 Shang Li Pien
Classification C-13 Philosophy + related subjects
Subject a book devoted to the defend of
         Confucianism from Buddhism.

References

Author 釋空谷景隆述 Shih Kung-Ku-Ching-Lung
Edition ①批駁本 ②抄寫本 ① Manuscript copy
         ③毛邊紙   ② "Mao-Pien" paper
         ④夢生庵主人藏 ⑤培經堂印
Index   ④ Mêng-Shêng-An, Chu-Jen Tsang
                        ⑤ Pei-Ching-Tang Ying printed
Bound in 1 tao   1 tsê

Remarks

297

. . . .

Accession No. 9 1401   Index No. 128-*kg*

Title 聯經 *Lien Ching*

Classification A 71

Subject *a collection of Chinese parallelism of*
對聯   *based on the ideas & words of*
Tuì Lien   *the classics*

References

Author 清李學禮(述) *Given in oral by*
                  Ching, Li Hsüeh-Li the blocks preserved edition

Edition 補過堂藏版 *Pu-Kuo-Táng Tsang Pan*

乾隆年刻 竹紙 *Dated, Chien-Lung period (1736-1795)*
Chien Lung Nien Kó *Chu Chih*
                       Bamboo paper

Index

Bound in 1 *Táo* 4 *chuan* 4 *Tsé.*

Remarks

The University of Toronto Chinese Library

. . . .

Accession No. 60 1402   Index No. 076-dhi

Title 欣賞編 Hsin Shang Pien

Classification C

Subject

References

Author 明 沈津編集 edited & Collected by Ming, Shēn Chin Pen Chi

Edition 明刻本 Ming Kó Pên Dated, Ming Dynastic (1368-1643)

Index

Bound in 1 tao 8 t'ie.

Remarks

The University of Toronto Chinese Library

. . . .

Accession No. *111* *1403*   Index No. *149-0 3/1 dggt*

Title 讀雪山房 唐詩鈔 *Tu Hsüeh Shan fang Tang Shih Chao*

Classification *D*

Subject

References

Author 清 管世銘 鈔 *Ching, Kuan Shih-Ming chao*

Edition 湖北官書處刊 *"Hu-Pei Kuan-Shu-Chü" Kan*
         光緒十二年刊 *Kuang Hsü Shih Êrh Nien Kan*
         Dated, Kuang-Hsü "Ping-Hsü" 12/1886

Index

Bound in *2 tao 34 chuan 12 tsé*

Remarks

300

The University of Toronto Chinese Library

. . . .

√ Accession No. ~~120~~ *1404*   Index No. 155-70-23

Title 赤牘清裁 *Chih Tu Ching Tsai*

Classification *D-73*

Subject *a collection of letters written by the important persons of the past.*

References

Author 明楊慎輯。 *Compiled by Ming, Yang-Shên ~~Chi~~*

Edition 明精刻本 *Ming, Ching Kê Pên Fine-printed*
         明白綿紙 *Ming, "Pai Mien ~~Chin~~ Chih paper*
                  Dated, Ming Dynastie (1368 – ~~1454~~)
                                              1643

Index

Bound in *1 tao 28 chuan 6 Tsê.*

Remarks

The University of Toronto Chinese Library
. . . .

73

Accession No. 1405   Index No. 0分-a 胡分升

Title   少室山房筆叢 Shao Shih Shan fang Pi Tsung

Classification   C

Subject

References

Author   明 胡應麟 撰 Written by ^ Ming, Hu Ying-Lin Chuan

Edition   廣雅書局刊 Kuang-Ya Shu Chü Kan Book Co.
          毛邊紙 "Mao-Pien" Chih paper

Index

Bound in   2 tao 48 chuan 12 tsé.

Remarks

The University of Toronto Chinese Library

. . . .

Accession No. 107 1406   Index No. 212-3ej-d

Title 龍泉園集 Lung Chüan Yüan Chi

Classification D

Subject

References

Author

Edition 家藏版 Private-family edition
                Chia Tsang Pan (Home Library)

        光緒年刻 毛邊紙
        Kuang Hsü Nien Kó "Mao Pien" chih paper

Index Dated, Kuang-Hsü period (1875-1908)

Bound in 2 tao   8 chuan 12 tsé.

Remarks

The University of Toronto Chinese Library

· ·

Accession No. 49 1407   Index No. 062-ablit

Title 戊戌履霜錄 Wu Hsü Lü ShuangLu

Classification C B-32

Subject An account of the political reformation happened in the year 1895(?) 戊戌
Wu Hsü

References

Author 退盧居士 Túi-Lu-Chü-Shih

Edition 退盧刊本 Túi-Lu Kán Pên block-printed edition.
豫章叢書本   白毛太紙
Yü-Chang Tsung Shu Pên. 'Pai-Mao-Tai' thin paper
separate edition from a Collectanea.

Index

Bound in 1 tao 6 chuan 3 tse.

Remarks

304

54

Accession No. *1408*   Index No. *042 998c*

Title   小窗艶紀   *Hsiao Chuang Yen Chi*

Classification   *C*

Subject

References

Author   明吳從先批選   *Selected by Ming, Wu Tsung-Hsien Pi Hsüan*

Edition   明刻本 *Ming, Kʻo Pên block-print edition*
          竹紙 *Chu Chih Bamboo paper*
          Dated   Ming Dynastie (1368-1643)

Index

Bound in   *1 tao 14 chuan 8 tsê.*

Remarks

The University of Toronto Chinese Library

. . . .

10

Accession No.　　1410　　　　　Index No. 031-53

Title　　四書　*Ssŭ Shu*

Classification　　A - 131　　The Four Books.

Subject

References

Author

Edition　　殿本　*Tien Pên Palace edition*
　　　　清國子監藏版　*Ching, Kuo Tzŭ-Chien Tsáng Pan blocks*　*Preserved ed.*

Index

Bound in　　1 tao　5 tsé.

Remarks

306

The University of Toronto Chinese Library

· ·

26

Accession No. 1411   Index No. 187-<del>dbsh</del>

Title 駱文忠公自訂年譜 *Lo Wên Chung Kung Tzŭ Ting Nien Pú*

Classification B

Subject

References

Author 清 駱秉章 撰 ^Written by Ching, Lo Ping-Chang <del>Chuan</del>

Edition 思賢書局重刊本 Ssŭ-Hsian Shu Chü Chung Kan Pên *reprinted*
Book Co. <del>Second</del> edition
光緒乙未年刊 *Dated:* Kuang-Hsü "I-Wei" Nien Kan 21/1895
毛邊紙 "Mao Pien" <del>Chih</del> paper

Index

Bound in 1 tao   2 chuan   2 tsé

Remarks

40

Accession No. 1412   Index No. 167. 九二0 月宇

Title 錢遵王讀書敏求記校証 Chien Tsun Wang Tu Shu Min Chiu
                                    chi Hsiao Ting Cheng

Classification B C-308

Subject

References

Author 清 管庭芳原輯   章鈺補輯 Compiled by
                                Ching, Kuan Ting-fang,
                                Chang Yü-Ba Chi.

Edition 長洲章氏刊 Chang-Chou, Chang-Shih Kan block-engraving.
        民國丙寅年刊 Ming-Kuo Ping Yin Nien Kan
        白毛邊紙 "Pai-Mao-Pien" thik paper

Index   Dated— 1926 (Ming-Kuo 15 Nien)

Bound in 1 tao 4 chuan 6 tsè.

Remarks

The University of Toronto Chinese Library

· ·

Accession No. 7 1413   Index No. 072-da Lc ...

Title 明本排字九經直音 *Ming Pên Pái Tzǔ Chiu Ching Chih Yin*

Classification A 166

Subject *A phonetic dictionary of g characters*
in the g classical book.

References

Author

Edition 清吳興陸氏十萬卷樓刻本 *Ching, Wu-Hsing Lu-Shih, Shih-I-Wan*
光緒七年刊 綿連紙   *Chüan-Lou Kʻo Pên*
Dated, Kuang-Hsü Chi Nien Kan "Mien-Lien" Chih paper
"Wu-Chên" 7/1868

Index

Bound in 1 *tao*   2 *tsê.*

Remarks

. . . .

Accession No. 89 1414   Index No. 030-dec7 kg

Title 呂祖直解金剛經 Lü Tsu Chih Chieh Chin Kang Ching

Classification C

Subject

References

Author 圓通文尼自在光佛直解 Yüan-Tʻung-Wên-Ni-Tzŭ-Tsai-Kuang-
                                      Fo Chih Chieh

Edition 北京龍雲齋藏版 Pei-Ching, Lung-Yün-Chai Tsang Pan block preserved ed.
         光緒庚辰年刊 Dated: Kuang-Hsü "Keng-Chʻen" Nien Kan 6/1880
         綿連紙 "Mien-Lien" Chih paper

Index

Bound in   1 tsê.

Remarks

The University of Toronto Chinese Library

. . . .

Accession No. 48 1415   Index No. 009-38

Title 傅 子 Fu Chuan Tzŭ

Classification C

Subject

References

Author 晉 傅 玄 撰 , Chin Written by Fu Chuan Hsüan Chuan

Edition 長沙葉氏刊 Cháng-Sha, Yeh-Shih Koo block-engraving.

Index

Bound in 1 t'ao 3 chuan 2 t'se.

Remarks

311

The University of Toronto Chinese Library

. . . .

127

Accession No. *1416*   Index No. *044-ЬPPƷ*

Title 屏廬叢刻 *Pin Lu Tsʹung Kʹo*

Classification   *C-336   Collections of Reprints*

Subject *A collection of several series of literary subjects such as poem stories, Painting of Plums, southern branch of*

References

Author

Edition 家藏版、 精刻本 綿連紙
Private family edition Home Library   *Fine-printed*   *Chia Tsʹang Pên*   *Ching Kʹo Pên*
"Mien-Lien" Chih paper

Index

Bound in   *2 tao   5 tśe*

Remarks

312

119

Accession No.   1417   Index No. 154-ec#dd

Title   貴池二妙集 Kuei Chih Êrh Miao Chi

Classification   C-338

Subject

References

Author   吳 吳應箕   劉 城 撰 Written by Wu, Wu Ying-Chi and Liu Chêng Chun

Edition   劉氏唐石簃彙刻 Liu-Shih, Táng-Shih-I Hui-Kó
白綿紙 "Pai-Mien" Chih paper

Index

Bound in   1 tao 51 Chuan 12 ts'e.

Remarks

313

. . . .

Accession No.   31   *1418*   Index No.   *189-AKOA*
                                                  33
                                                 053-jck

Title   高士傳續編   廉吏傳   *Kao Shih Chuan Hsü Pien*
                                Lien Li Chuan

Classification   *B*

Subject

References

Author   清張允掄著 *ching, Chang Yün-Lun* ~~Cta~~

Edition   新城縣署刊本 *Hsing-Chêng, Hsien Shu Kan Pên*
          Dated: *"Ping-Shen" 22/1896*
          光緒二十二年刊 *Kuang-Hsü Erh Shih Erh Nien Kan*
          洋粉連紙 *"Yang-fên-Lien" ~~Cith~~ paper*

Index

Bound in   1 t'ao   6 chuan   6 t'sè.

Remarks   1 t'ao   6 chuan   6 t'se.

The University of Toronto Chinese Library

. . . .

85

Accession No.   1419   Index No. 041-刧刧

Title   封氏聞見記 Fêng Shih Wên Chien Chi

Classification C - 308

Subject Miscellaneous writings, discussions
+ expositions on Confucianism,
classics + Morals.

References

Author 唐 封演 Tang, Fêng Yen

Edition 江都秦氏刊 Chiang-Tu, Chin-Shih Kán published block engraving.
乾隆年刻   綿紙 Chien-Lung Nien Kô period (1936-1995)
                                    "Mien" paper
夷山王氏藏 I-Shan, Wang-Shih Tsang edited
Index   — Table of Contents

Bound in 1 tao   10 chuan   2 tie.

Remarks

315

. . . .

76-AB

Accession No.   1420 A-B   Index No. 009-egb

Title 佛說四十二章經解 Fo Shueh Ssŭ Shih Ênh Chang Ching Chieh

Classification

Subject

References

Author 明釋智旭撰 *Written by* Ming, Shih Chih-Hsü Chuan

Edition 京都廣慧寺重校梓 *Re-rivised* Ching-Tu, Kuang-Hui-Ssŭ Chung Hsiao Tzǔ

竹紙 Chu Chih *Bamboo Paper*

Index

Bound in 1 tao   2 tsĕ.

Remarks

316

The University of Toronto Chinese Library

. . . .

112

Accession No. 1421   Index No. 069-inh

Title 新疆賦 Hsin Chiang Fu

Classification D 103

Subject A lyrical description of Shikiang.

References

Author 清徐松撰。 Written by Ching, Hsü Sung Chuan

Edition 家藏版 Chia Tsang Pan Home Library Private family edition
綿連紙 "Mien-Lien" Chih paper

Index

Bound in 1 tao 1 tse.

Remarks

317

The University of Toronto Chinese Library

....

Accession No. *80* *1422*   Index No. *120-mc*

Title 繹畜志 *I Chih*

Classification *C 13*

Subject *A 19-volume work dealing with various philosophical subjects.*

References

Author 明 胡承諾譔 *Ming, Hu Chêng-No Chuan*

Edition 三餘草堂藏版 *"San-Yü-Tsao" Tang Tsang* *block preserved edition* *Pan Heme Library*
光緒辛卯年刻 *Dated Kuang-Hsü "Hsin-Mao" Nien Kó* *17/1891*
毛邊紙 *"Mao-Pien" Chih paper*

Index *Table of contents*

Bound in *1 Tao 19 Chuan 8 Tóe*

Remarks

318

The University of Toronto Chinese Library

....

78

Accession No. 1423   Index No. 123-盦ph

Title 羣言瀝液 Chün Yen Li Yeh

Classification C - 13

Subject a collection of quotations

References

Author 清 梁顗祖 彙編, edited by Ching, Liang Hsien-Tsu Hui Pien

Edition ~~Home library~~ private family edition
         "Mao-pien" paper

Index

Bound in 1 tao 8 chuan 4 tsé

Remarks

319

The University of Toronto Chinese Library

. . . .

Accession No. 127 1424   Index No. 181-gbLn 外

Title   賴古堂藏書 Lai Ku Tang Tsang Shu

Classification   C-338

Subject

References

Author   清 周在梁 輯 Compiled by Ching, Chou Tsai-Liang Edi

Edition   賴古堂 版 "Lai-Ku-Tang Pan
             共十三種 Kung Shih San Chung All to-gether 13 kinds
             竹紙 Chu Chih Bamboo paper

Index

Bound in   1 tao 4 tse

Remarks

320

The University of Toronto Chinese Library

. . . .

112

Accession No. *1425*   Index No. *030-七八六六*

Title   商文毅公集 *Shang Wên I Kung Chi*

Classification   *山文毅集 D-*

Subject

References

Author   明商文毅公撰   明張一魁編
Written by Ming ShangWên-I-Kung Chuan edited by Ming, Chang I-Kuei Pien
Edition   七世孫商德協刊   *Chi-Shih-Sun, Shang Tê Hsieh Kan*

順治十五年刊 *Shun Chih Shih Wu Nien Kan*
Dated, Shun-Chih "Wu-Hsü" 15/1658

Index

Bound in   1 tao   6 Chuan   4 tsê

Remarks

The University of Toronto Chinese Library

. . . .

69

Accession No.   1426   Index No. 061-icgh

Title   愚齋語錄 *Yü Chai Yü Lu*

Classification   C -13

Subject   An exposition of Confucianism with
references with other writings &
Buddhist doctrines.

References

Author   清熊孝昌著 *Ching, Hsiung Hsiao-Chang Chu*

Edition   敬業山房藏版 *"Ching-Yeh-Shan-fang" Tsang Pan block preserved.*
ed.
康熙年刻   竹紙 *Kang Hsi Nien Ko* Chu Chih
Bamboo Paper
Dated, Kang-Hsi period (1662-1722

Index

Bound in   1 tao   3 chuan   2 tse

Remarks

The University of Toronto Chinese Library

. . . .

59

Accession No. *1427*   Index No. *162-legz*

Title   選註孫子 *Chuan Chu Sun Tzŭ*

Classification   *C -*

Subject

References

Author   夏壽田選註 *Annotated by Hsia Shou-Tien* ~~Sh Hsüan Chu~~

Edition   碌絲格石印大字 *Chu Ssŭ Ko Shih Yin Ta Tzu*
          Lithographic ~~edition~~ *large character edition.*

Index

Bound in   *1 Tao   2 Tsè.*

Remarks

323

The University of Toronto Chinese Library

. . . .

30

Accession No. *1428*   Index No. -*085- hbje*
                                        085 - hbje th

"Shun-Hua Ko t'eh Shih Wen"

Title 淳化閣帖釋文 *Ch'un Hua Ko Tieh Shih Wen*

Classification β-347日錄 — 金石 *Chin Shih*

Subject - explanatory notes on the Shun-Hua specimens of handwriting.

References 012-gafk 9/22. Toronto No. 33/

Author 清朱家標釋 *Ch'ing, Chu Chia-Piao Shih*
                    Explained by

Edition 絅錦堂版 *"K'ang Chin-T'ang" Pan blocks*
                    Tung

Index

Bound in 1 tao 10 Chuan 2 ts'e.

Remarks

324

The University of Toronto Chinese Library

. . . .

15

Accession No.　1429　　　Index No. 170-陳叔

Title　陳氏 中西 回史 日曆 Ch'en Shih Chukng Hsi Hui Shih Jih Li

Classification　B-1.57

Subject　C Calendar g both Chinese
　　　　historical
　　　　^
　　　　& Mohamadan histories.
　　　　events.

References

Author　陳垣 撰 Ch'en Yuan-Ch'an
　　　　Written by y
　　　　^

Edition　國立北京 大學研究所 國學門叢刊.
Kuo Li Pei-Ching Ta Hsueh Yen Chiu Só　Kuo Hsueh Mên Tsung Kan
(Peiking University, China)

Index

Bound in　1 tao　20 Chuan　5 tsé.

Remarks

325

The University of Toronto Chinese Library

....

Accession No.   ⁷⁰ 1430   Index No. 021 - 清卿

Title   北山錄 Pei Shan Lu

Classification   C 513 Buddhism

Subject   An exposition on Buddhist doctrine
+ practices by a monk of the Sung
Dynasty with notes.

References

Author   宋釋神清撰 _{Written by} Sung, Shih Shen-Ching Chuan

Edition   宋熙寧元年 影刻本 _{Photo-lithographic edition} Sung, Hsi Ning Yuan Nien Ying Kó Pên
白洋毛邊紙 "Pai-Yang-Mao-Pien" Chih paper
Dated, Sung, Hsi-Ning "Wu-Shen" 1/1068

Index

Bound in ^{1 tao} 12 Chuan 在 4 tsê

Remarks

326

The University of Toronto Chinese Library

. . . .

Accession No.   1431   Index No. 072-da he cege

Title 明本排字九経直音 Ming Pên Pái Tzŭ Chiu Ching Chih Yin

Classification A

Subject

References

Author

Edition 清吳興陸氏十萬卷樓刻本 Ching, Wu-Hsing Lu Shih
         光緒七年刊 Kuang Hsü Chi Nien Kan   Shih Wan Chüan Lou Ko Pên
         錦連紙 "Mien-Lien" Chih paper
Index   Dated, Kuang-Hsü "Hsing-Szu" 7/1881

Bound in 1 tao   2 tsè

Remarks

．．．．．．．．．．．．．．．．．．．．．

1 1431

Accession No. ~~1620~~   Index No. 089-jdzk

Title 爾雅音圖 *Êrh Ya Yin Tu*

Classification A-156

Subject

References

Author 晉郭璞註 ∧ *Annotated by Chin, Kuo Pu*

Edition 影宋大字本 ~~this~~ *Photo-Lithographic ed from Sung ed.*
in big letters

嘉慶六年辛酉藝學軒摹刊

Dated, Chia-Ching "Hsien-Yu" 6/1801

Index

Bound in 1 *tao*, 2 *ts'ê*

Remarks

328

84

Accession No. *1432*   Index No. *140-9329*

Title 莊子正義 *Chuang Tzŭ Chêng I*

Classification *C-1432 731*

Subject

References

Author 清 陳壽昌 輯 *Compiled by* *Ching, Chên Shou-Chang*

Edition 怡顏齋刊 *I-Yen-Chai Kan block engraving.*
光緒十九年刻 *Dated,* *"Keei-Szŭ" 19/1893* *Kuang-Hsü Shih Chiu Nien Kê*
綿連紙 *"Mien-Lien" Paper*

Index

Bound in 1 *tao*   6 *tse*

Remarks

. . . .

Accession No. *18* 1433   Index No. 024-36he

Title 十六國春秋 *Shih Liu Kuo Ch'un Chiu*

Classification B-117 *Collected biographies*

Subject *a collection of biographies of the 16 ~~Kingdoms~~ dynasties ~~during~~ edited from Book of Wei (魏書)*
                                                        "Wei Shu"

References

Author 魏 崔鴻撰 *Written by Wei, Tsui Hung*

Edition 家藏版 *~~Home Library~~ Private family edition*
        毛太紙 *"Mao-Tai" paper*

Index

Bound in *1 tao   4 chuan   4 tse*

Remarks

330

The University of Toronto Chinese Library

. . . .

Accession No. 117 1434   Index No. 120-03hg

Title   女- 續玉臺文苑 *Hsü Yü Tái Wên Yüan*

Classification D-73 *Prose.*

Subject   *A collection of prose, essays, letters*
&c. written by women of the different
dynasties.

References   *edited & compiled by*

Author   明 江元祚 編輯。 *Ming, Chiang Yüan-Tsu*

Edition 明崇禎壬申年刊本 *Dated, Ming, Chung-Chên "Jen-Shen"*
                                                    5/1632
         竹紙 *Bamboo paper*

Index

Bound in   1 *tao*   4 *chuan*   4 *tsê*

Remarks

. . . .

63

Accession No.   1435   Index No. 096-993m

Title   琉球入學見聞錄 Liu Chiu Ju Hsüeh Chien Wên Lu

Classification   ℚ B-196 Tributary States

Subject   a book on 琉球 with geographical,
"Liu Chiu";
social & educational description

References

Author   潘相輯, Pan Hsiang
                Compiled by

Edition   毛氏汲古閣版 Mao-Shih-Chi-Ku-Ko Pan blocks.
竹紙 Bamboo paper

Index

Bound in   1 tao 1 Chuan 2 tse

Remarks

The University of Toronto Chinese Library

. . . .

28

Accession No. *1436*   Index No. *001-bdhe*

Title 三希堂法帖釋文 *San Hsi Tang Fa Teh Shih Wen*

Classification *B*

Subject

References

Author

Edition 清殿版 *Ching, Tien Pan Palace edition*
乾隆年刻) *Dated, Chien-Lung period (1036-1795)*

Index

Bound in *1 Tao   16 Chuan   8 Ts'e*

Remarks

The University of Toronto Chinese Library

. . . .

67

Accession No.   1437   Index No. 140·dqhg

Title 花陣綺言 Hua Chên I Yen

Classification C - 388 387 Colloquial Novels

Subject A love Story

References

Author 楚江仙隱石公纂輯 Compiled by Chu-Chiang Hsien-Yin Shih-Kung

Edition 明刻本 Dated, Ming, Dynastie (1368—1644)
竹紙 Bamboo paper

Index

Bound in 1 tao   2 tse.

Remarks

. . . .

24

Accession No. *1438*   Index No. *040-dahe*

Title 宋本韓柳二先生年譜 *Sung Pên Han Liu Ênh Hsien Sheng Nien Pú*

Classification *β*

Subject

References

Author 宋 呂大防輯 *Compiled by Sung, Lü Ta-Fang*

Edition 小玲瓏山館 仿宋重刋 *Hsiao-Ling-Lung-Shan-Kuon Fang Sung Chóng Kèn reprinted ed.*
雍正年刻 竹紙 *Bamboo Paper*

Index *Dated, Yung-Chêng period (1723-1735)*

Bound in *1 tao 8 chuan 2 t'se.*

Remarks

335

69

Accession No.   1439   Index No. 085- 9oze

Title   海瓊白真人語錄   Hai Chʻiung Pai Chên Jên Yü Lu

Classification   C -731   Taoism

Subject   a collection of a Taoist monk sayings

References

Author   道士 謝顯道編,   edited by "Tao-Shih" Hsieh Hsien-Tao

Edition   抄寫本   Manuscript copy.
          白綿紙 "Pai-Mien" paper

Index   None

Bound in   1 tao   2 tse.

Remarks

336

The University of Toronto Chinese Library

. . . .

Accession No. 39 1440   Index No. 008-7363

Title 京口三山志 Ching K'ou San Shan Chih

Classification B

Subject

References

Author 清 周伯義編 edited by Ching. Chou Po-I

Edition 局版 Chü Pan

光緒年刻 毛邊紙
"Mao-Pien" paper
Dated, Kuang-Hsü period (1875-1908).

Index

Bound in   3 Tao   全山志   20 Chuan
                       焦山志   26   "
Remarks   續志   8   "
                       固山志   14   "

337

Cab I

11

Accession No. 1441   Index No. 077-ajic

Title 正韻辨字全書 *Chêng Yün Pien Tzŭ Chüan Shu*

Classification A

Subject

References

Author

Edition 舊狄本 *Old Manuscript copy*

白 紙 *pei White paper*

Index

Bound in 1 Tao 2 Chuan 2 Tsê.

Remarks

338

. . . .

36

Accession No.   *1442*   Index No. *196-chei*

Title 鳳臺祇謁筆記 *Fêng Tái Chih Yeh Pi Chi*

Classification   *B-222 Voyages & Travels.*

Subject *A descriptive account of the points of*
interests round Feng Tai

References

Author 清熙和梭刊本 *Ching, Hsi Ho Hsiao K'an Pên blak print ed.*

Edition 同治庚午年刊 *Dated, T'ung-Chih "Kêng-Wu" 9/1870*
竹紙 *Bamboo paper*

Index

Bound in *1 t'ao   2 ts'e*

Remarks

Accession No.   *127*   *1443*   Index No. *061- ㄒㄧㄣCP*

Title   惜陰軒叢書續編   *Hsi Yin Hsüan Tsung Shu Hsü Pien*

Classification   *C-338*

Subject

References

Author   清 王沿等輯   *Compiled by*
                         Ching, Wang Chih

Edition   宏道書院藏版   *"Hung-Tao-Shu-Yüan" Tsang Pan*   *blocks preserved ed.*
           毛邊紙   *"Mao-Pien" paper*

Index

Bound in   *1 Tao 9 Tse*

Remarks

The University of Toronto Chinese Library
....

Accession No. 69 *1444*   Index No. *140-dzjj*

Title 芥子園畫傳 *Chieh Tzŭ Yüan Hua Chuan*

Classification *C-*

Subject

References

Author 王安節摹古 *Wang An Chieh*

Edition 芥子園刊 *Chieh-Tzŭ-Yüan Kan block-engraving.*
康熙年刻 粉紙 *Dated, Kang-Hsi period (1662-1724)*
"Fên" Paper

Index

Bound in *1 tao   5 chuan   5 tsě.*

Remarks

The University of Toronto Chinese Library

. . . .

120

Accession No. *1445*   Index No. *012-bb38*

Title 六朝文絜 *Liu Chao Wen Chie*

Classification D

Subject

References

Author 清 許 璉 評選 *Commented & Selected by: Ching, Hsü Lien*

Edition 讀有用書齋刊 *Tu-Yu-Yung-Shu-Chai Kan*
碟批評點 *Commentories Printed in Red*

Index

Bound in 1 tao 4 chuan 2 tse.

Remarks

342

． ． ． ． ． ． ． ． ． ． ． ． ． ． ． ． ． ．

Accession No. 49 *1446*   Index No. 024-gdbg

Title 南省公餘錄 *Nan Shêng Kung Yü Lu*

Classification *C - 308*

Subject *Miscellaneous writing on governmental offices & officers.*

References

Author 清 梁章鉅 撰 *Written by Ching, Liang Chang-Chü*

Edition 家藏版 *Home Library Private family edition*
夾連紙 *"Chia-Lien" paper*

Index

Bound in *1 Tao   4 Chuan   2 Tsé*

Remarks

343

. . . .

Accession No.　　*11*　　*1447*　　Index No. *120-gk* ${}_{m}^{le}$

Title　經傳釋詞 *Ching Chuan Shih Tzŭ*

Classification　*A*

Subject

References

Author　清 王引之著 *Ching, Wang Yin-Chih*

Edition　文學山房聚珍版印
Wên-Hsüeh-Shan ~~Feng Chü Chen~~ Pan Yin Movable-type edition

Index

Bound in　*1 tao　10 Chuan　4 tsé*

Remarks

344

The University of Toronto Chinese Library
· ·

12

Accession No.   *1448*   Index No. 064-deeg

Title   批點尚書讀本 *Pi Tien Shang Shu Tu Pên*

Classification   A

Subject

References

Author   清   王言綸批點   *Commented & Punctuated by*
    Ching, Wang Yen Lun Pi Tien

Edition   精鈔原刻底本 *Fine Manuscript from the Original edition*
    硃批點.   山西紙   *Commentaries Printed in Red*
    "Shan-Hsi" paper

Index

Bound in   1 tao   6 chuan   6 tse.

Remarks

The University of Toronto Chinese Library

. . . .

15

Accession No.   *1449*   Index No. *149 - edze*

Title   詞林典故 *Tʒʾü Lin Tien Ku*

Classification   *B - 257 (?)*

Subject

References

Author   清 張廷玉等修輯。 *Compiled by* *Ching, Chang Tíng Yü*

Edition   殿版 *"Tien Pan Palace edition"*
竹
乾隆戊辰年刻 厚紙
^
Thick Bamboo paper
Index   *Dated, Chʾien-Lung "Wu Hsü-Chʾen "13/1948*

Bound in   *1 tao   8 chuan   10 ts̆e.*

Remarks

. . . .

107

Accession No.   *1450*   Index No. *170-LPai*

Title 陶廬百篇 *Tao Lu Pai Pien*

Classification   *D 43*

Subject *a collection of essays on various topics by Wang Shae-Shan*

References

Author 王樹枬 撰 *Written by Wang Shu-Nan*

Edition 吉林成氏十三古槐館刊 *Chi-Lin, Chêng Shih, Shih-San-Ku-Huai-Kuan (Kan)*
民國十四年刻, 硃色, 初次精印 *First edition, Fine-printed in Red*
夾連紙 *"Chia-Lien" Chih*

Index   *Dated, Ming-Kuo 14 Nien 1925*

Bound in

Remarks

The University of Toronto Chinese Library

. . . .

49

Accession No.   1451   Index No. 075-dedh

Title   東周列國志 Tung Choa Lieh Kuo Chih.

Classification   C

Subject

References

Author   清蔡元放批評   Commented by
                        Ching, Tsai Yüan-Fang

Edition 書成山房刻 珠套版   Shu-Chêng-Shan-fang Kó
                              Chu-Táo Pan
         咸豐四年刻，竹 紙
                        Bamboo paper
Index   Dated, Hsien-Têng "Chia-Ying" 4/1854

Bound in   1 Tao   12 Tsê

Remarks

. . . .

Accession No. 57
1452   Index No. 032-jg

Title 墊說 Tú H̶s̶i̶e̶h̶ Shuo

Classification C - 308

Subject Miscellaneous writings, prose + poems

References

Author 清 繆 蓮 仙 輯 Compiled by Ching, Miao Lien-Hsien

Edition 如此草堂 版 "Ju-Tśg-Tśao-Táng" Raw blocks.
道光年刻 Dated, Tao-Kuang period (1821~1850)
毛邊紙 "Maopien" paper

Index

Bound in 1 tao   4 chuan   4 tśe

Remarks

Accession No. 64 1453   Index No. 021-cdj3

Title 北東園筆錄全集 *Pei Tung Yüan Pi Lu Chüan Chi*

Classification C

Subject

References

Author 清 梁恭辰 選述 *Selected & given in Oral by Ching, Liang Kung-Chen*

Edition 不媿屋漏齋主人重刊本 *Pu-Kúei-Wu Lou-Chai Chu jen Chúng Kan Pén reprinted Second edition*
光緒二十年刊 綿連紙 *Dated, Kuang-Hsü "Chia-Wu" "Mien-Lien" paper 20/1894*

Index

Bound in 1 *Tao* 24 *Chuan* 8 *Tse*.

Remarks

. . . .

66

Accession No.   1454   Index No. 149-LL

Title 談 徵 *Tán Chêng*

Classification   C-510   Folk-lore.

Subject a collection of ~~short stories on different~~ folk-lore in the form of short stories.

References

Author 外方山人 輯 *Compiled by Wai-fang-Shan-gên*

Edition 上苑堂藏版 *Shang-Yuen Tang block preserved ed.*
道光三年鐫 *Dated, Tao-Kuang "Kuei-Wei" 3/1823*
毛邊紙 *"Mao-pien" paper*

Index

Bound in 1 tao 函 5 tsè

Remarks

351

The University of Toronto Chinese Library

. . . .

72

Accession No.   *1455*   Index No. *009-ndbb*

Title   儒林外史 *Ju Lin Wai Shih*

Classification   *C- 387 Colloquial Novels.*

Subject   *a Chinese novels on literary
people*

References

Author   清 吳敬梓 撰 *Written by Ching, Wu Ching-Tzŭ*

Edition   齊省堂藏版 *Chi-San-Tong block preserved ed.*
同治年刻 *Dated, Tung-Chih period (1862-1874)*

Index

Bound in   *2 tao   12 tsé.*

Remarks   *2 sets*

The University of Toronto Chinese Library

. . . .

Accession No. *61* *1456*   Index No. *069-igh*

Title 新義錄 *Hsin I Lu*

Classification *C*

Subject

References

Author 清 孫璧文 輯 *Compiled by* *Ching, Sun Pi-Wên*

Edition 漱石山房藏版 *Sou-Shih-Shan-Fang* *block preserved ed.* *print-printed* 光緒丙辰年墻本 *Dated, Kuang-Hsü "Ping-Chên"*

Index

Bound in *4 tao 100 Chuan 40 tse.*

Remarks

. . . .

40

Accession No. *1457*   Index No. *162-gnk手*

Title 通鑑總類 *Tûng Chien Tsung Lei*

Classification *B.*

Subject

References

Author 清沈鼎輯。 *Compiled by Ching, Shên Yü*

Edition 讀我書齋刊 *Tu-Wo-Shu-Chai published blocks.*
重刻元本 *Re-engraved the Yüan edition*

Index

Bound in *4 Tao 20 Chuan 20 Tse.*

Remarks

354

The University of Toronto Chinese Library

. . . .

Accession No.   *58*   1458   Index No. 042-zmez

Title   小學紺珠 *Hsiao Hsüeh Kan Chu*

Classification   C-348 Encyclopedias

Subject   a Dictionary on terms of numbers, histories & others.

References

Author   宋王應麟著 *Sung, Wang Ying-Lin*

Edition   家藏版 ~~Home Library~~ Private Family edition
同治十二年刻 Dated, Tung-Chih "Kuei-Yu" 12/1873
粉紙 "Fěn" paper

Index   Table of Contents

Bound in   1 tao   10 Chuan   6 tsé

Remarks

355

. . . .

Accession No. 64 1459   Index No. 040-Ljhd

Title 寄園寄所寄 Chi Yüan Chi So Chi

Classification C

Subject

References

Author 清.趙吉士著 Ching, Chao Chi-Shih

Edition 姑蘇文秀堂藏版 Ku-Su, Wên-Hsiu-Tang private printed block preserved ed.

竹紙 Bamboo Paper

Index

Bound in   12 Chuan   12 Tsé.

Remarks

356

The University of Toronto Chinese Library

. . . .

Accession No.   55
                 1460   Index No. 120-llck

Title   繡像紅樓夢 Hsiu Hsiang Hung Lou Mêng

Classification   C-368

Subject

References

Author   清 曹雪芹著 Ch'ing, Tsao Hsüeh Chin

Edition   京都聚珍堂印 Ching-Tu, Movable-type editions Chü-Chên-Tang published

Index

Bound in   1 tao   120 chuan   24 tsê

Remarks

The University of Toronto Chinese Library

. . . .

58

Accession No. _1461_   Index No. 042-gch

Title 小知錄 Hsiao Chih Lu

Classification C-348

Subject

References

Author 清 陸鳳藻著 Ching, Lu Fêng-Tsao

Edition 琴雅堂版 Chên-Ya-Tâng blocks.
嘉慶年刻 白毛邊紙 夾版 wooden folder.
"Pai-Mao-Pien" paper
Dated, Chia-Ching period (1796-1820)

Index

Bound in 2 Tao   12 Chuan   12 Tsê.

Remarks

The University of Toronto Chinese Library

. . . .

56

Accession No.   1462   Index No. 164-cccg

Title 酌中志餘 Cho Chung Chih Yü

Classification   C - 348

Subject A book consists of several lists of rebels, + unofficial heroes.

References

Author 野史氏 Yeh-Shih Shih

Edition 家藏版 ~~Home Library~~ Private family edition
绵連纸 "Mien-Lien" paper
夾板 Wood-block

Index

Bound in   1 Tao 2 Chuan 2 tse

Remarks

359

. . . .

16

Accession No.   1463   Index No. 031-bgnc

Title 四裔編年表 Ssŭ I Pien Nien Piao

Classification   B - 157

Subject a historical chart comparison dates
in the important ~~events~~ happenings
between Chinese + the world
~~this~~ chronologies.

References

Author 美國林樂知 中國嚴良勳譯 李鳳苞彙編
Lin Lo-Chih (U.S.A.), Yen Liang- Shün and Li Fêng-Pao edited.
translated

Edition Lithographic Version.

毛邊紙. "Mao-Pien" paper

Index

Bound in   1 tao 4 tsé

Remarks

The University of Toronto Chinese Library

· ·

82

Accession No.   *1464*   Index No. *128-ecc3*

Title   聊齋志異圖詠 *Liao Chai Chih I Tu Yüng*

Classification   *C - 387 368*

Subject   *a poetical appreciation on* 聊齋
with pictures.

References

Author

Edition   *Kuang-Pai-Sung-Chai*
廣百宋齋本   連史紙 *"Lien-Shih" paper*
同文書局石印   夾板 *Wood-block*
T'ung-Wén Book Co. Lithographic ed.

Index   *Table of contents*

Bound in   *1 tao   16 chuan   4 tsé*

Remarks

The University of Toronto Chinese Library

. . . .

Accession No.　120　1465　　　Index No. 060-khze

Title　御製文初集 Yü Chih Wên Chu Chi

Classification　D

Subject

References

Author　清嘉慶帝選 Selested by Ching, Chia-Ching Emperor

Edition　殿本版中箱本 Palace ed. Pocket-ed.
綿連紙 "Mien-Lien" paper

Index

Bound in　1 tao　10 chüan　8 tsê.

Remarks

. . . .

Accession No. 73 *1466*   Index No. *030-bg3*

Title 古事比 *Ku Shih Pi*

Classification *C - 348*

Subject *A book composed of historical accounts of interest illustrating human relationships.*

References

Author 清 方中德 輯著 *Compiled by Ching, Fang Chung-Tê*

Edition 點石齋石印 *Lithographic Version* 光緒十三年印 連史紙 *"Lien-Shih" paper Dated, Kuang-Hsü "Ting-Hai" 13/1887*

Index *Table of Contents Bibliography*

Bound in *1 tao 52 Chuan 6 tsê*

Remarks

The University of Toronto Chinese Library

. . . .

55 本

Accession No. *1467*   Index No. *167-kdi*

Title   鏡花錄 *Ching Hua Yüan*

Classification   *C - 368* 小說家

Subject

References

Author   清李汝珍著 *Ching, gu Li gu-chên*

Edition   點石齋印 *Dien-Shih-Chai published*
   光緒十四年印 *Dated, Kuang-Hsü "Wu-Tzü" 14/1888*
   粉紙 夾板. *Wood-block*

Index   *"fên" paper*

Bound in   *1 tao*   *6 tse*

Remarks

364

. . . .

Accession No. 89 1468   Index No. 018-d7在n

Title 刑案滙覽 Hsing An Hui Lan

Classification C

Subject

References

Author 清 鮑春芸參定 \ edited in order by 祝慶祺編次
Ching Pao Chun-Yün   Chu Ching-Chi

Edition 圖書集成局 仿袖珍本印 Pocket edition.

連史紙 鉛印 Type-setting edition.
Zien-Shih" paper

Index

Bound in 4 tao 60 chuan 40 tse.

Remarks

365

The University of Toronto Chinese Library

. . . .

52 ~~典~~

Accession No.   1469   Index No. 039-a399

Title   孔子家語 Kʻung Tzŭ Chia Yü

Classification C

Subject

References

Author   魏王肅註 Wei, Wang Su ∧Annotated by

Edition   上海 同文書局 影內府藏本 Ying-Nei-Fu private-printed
Shanghai, Tung-Wên Book Co.
綿連紙 Shanghai, Tung Wên Book Co. Ying Nei Fu preserved ed.
"Mien-Lien" paper

Index

Bound in   1 tao   10 Chuan   5 tsê.

Remarks

366

The University of Toronto Chinese Library

. . . .

Accession No. · 28頁 1470   Index No. 001-b93i

Title 三通攷輯要 San Tung Kao Chi Yao

Classification B -

Subject

References

Author 清 湯壽潛 編輯 edited & compiled by Ching, Táng Shou-Chien

Edition 圖書集成局 鉛印本 Type-setting ed.
光緒二十五年 Dated, Kuang-Hsü "Chi-Hai" 25/1899
己亥

Index

Bound in 6 tao 60 tze

Remarks

367

The University of Toronto Chinese Library
. . . .

Accession No. 1471   Index No. 118-e3苦

Title 第一才子書 Ti I Ts'ai Tzŭ Shu

Classification C-368

Subject

References

Author 聖嘆外書 毛宗闓評 Commented by Mao Tsung-Kang.

Edition Shêng Han Wai Shu

Index

Bound in 1 Tao, 8 Ts'ê

Remarks

The University of Toronto Chinese Library

....

54 才

Accession No. 1472   Index No. 118-e388

Title   第一才子書 Ti I Ts'ai Tzŭ Shu

Classification   C-368

Subject

References

Author   聖嘆外書   毛宗岡評
         Shêng Han Wai Shu   Mao Tsung-Kang

Edition 羣玉山房刊硃批
         Chün-Yu-Shan-Fang ed. Commentaries in red

Index   2

Bound in   2 tao 60 Chuan 20 tsé.

Remarks

The University of Toronto Chinese Library

. . . .

Accession No. 1473   Index No.

Title 花月痕全書 Hua Yüeh Hen Chüan Shu

Classification

Subject

References

Author 清眠鶴道人撰 Written by Ching, Mian Ho Tao Jen

Edition 閩雙笏廬藏版 Fukien, Shuang Hu Lu blok preserved
光緒戊子年刊 綿連紙 夾板 wooden block.
Dated: Kuang Hsü Wu Tzu "mien Lien" paper

Index

Bound in 16 tsê

Remarks

370

. . . .

110

Accession No.   1474   Index No. 106-dhgd

Title   皇朝經世文新編 Huang Chào Ching Shih Nên Hsing Pien

Classification   D

Subject

References

Author   清 麥仲華 輯 Compiled by Ching. Mai Chung-Hua

Edition   上海大同譯書局石印
Shang-Hai "Ta-Tung I Shu Chü" lithographie ed.
(Book Co.)

Index

Bound in   2 tao 21 chuan 24 tse.

Remarks

60

Accession No. 1475   Index No. 149-jhhb

Title 謝華啓秀 Hsieh Hua Chi Hsiu

Classification C-348 Encyclopedias

Subject An encyclopedias of Chinese phrases
+ terms in literature.

References

Author 明楊慎編 edited by Ming. Yang Shên

Edition 戹敬齋藏版 Kao-Ching-Chai private printed block preserved ed.
綿連紙 "Mien-Lien" paper

Index

Bound in 1 tao 6 tsê.

Remarks

372

84

Accession No.   1476   Index No. 040-ㅁjㅅㅅ

Title   寄園寄所寄   Chi Yüan Chi So Chi

Classification   C

Subject

References

Author   清 趙吉士 著   Ching Chao Chi-Shih

Edition   竹紙   Bamboo paper

Index

Bound in   2 tao,   12 chuan   6 tsê.

Remarks

The University of Toronto Chinese Library

. . . .

126

Accession No. *1477*   Index No. *118- Z g 38*

Title   算經十書 *Suan Ching Shih Shu*

Classification   *C 338*

Subject

References

Author   魏 劉 徽 等 註 *Annotated by Wei, Liu Hui*

Edition   上海 鴻寶齋石印本 *Shanghai, Hung-Pao-Chai lithographic ed.*
光緒丙申年印 洋粉連紙 *"Yang-Fên-Lien" paper*
Dated, Kuang-Hsü "Ping-Shen" 22/1896

Index

Bound in   *1 tao   24 chuan   8 ts'e.*

Remarks

The University of Toronto Chinese Library

. . . .

49

Accession No.   1478   Index No. 120-0Ckk

Title   續紅樓夢 Hsü Hung Lou Mêng

Classification   C -35⁊368

Subject

References

Author

Edition   抱甕軒版 Pao-Wêng-Hsien ed.
                                        Hsüan
          嘉慶乙未刻 白毛太紙
                      "Pai-Mao-Tai" paper
          崇雲卿父藏 Chúng-Yün Ching-Shih private printed
                                                    Preserved

Index

Bound in   2 tao   30 Chuan   18 tsé.

Remarks

375

. . . .

49

Accession No. 1479   Index No. 032-2g义h

Title 增補類腋 Tsêng Pu Lei Yeh

Classification C-348 Encyclopedias

Subject An encyclopedias on Heaven, Earth, subjects connected with the personalities, writers, cooking +c.

References

Author 清 趙克宣 增輯, Compiled by Ching, Chao Kó-I

Edition 南山樓版 Chio-Shan-Lou-ed.

Index with detailed table of contents

Bound in 2 tao 20 tsé.

Remarks

376

The University of Toronto Chinese Library

. . . .

Accession No. 20
1480   Index No. 140-いとbe

Title 萬國公法 Wan Kuo Kung Fa

Classification B

Subject

References

Author 清丁韙良譯 Ching, Ting Wei-Liang translated

Edition 鉛印本 Type-setting ed.

Index

Bound in 1 tao 4 chuan 4 tée.

Remarks

Accession No.   *119*   *1481*   Index No. 024-g33d

Title   南山文集 *Nan Shan Wên Chi*

Classification D

Subject

References

Author 清戴潛虛著 *Ching, Tai Chien Hsü*

Edition 家藏版 ~~Home Library~~ *Private family edition*

Index

Bound in 1 tao   16 chuan   8 tśe.

Remarks

Accession No.　29　1482　　　　Index No. 120-cbi

Title　紀元編　Chi Yüan Pien

Classification　B-157

Subject　a book of chronology on Chinese dynasties & Emperors.

References

Author

Edition　粵雅堂叢書本　Yüeh-Ya-Tang Tsüng Shu Pên　separata edition from a collectanea

竹紙, 夾板　Wood-block
Bamboo paper

Index

Bound in　1 tao　3 chuan　3 tse

Remarks

· ·

58

Accession No. *1483*   Index No. *001-dgig*

Title 世說新語補 *Shih Shuo Hsin Yü Pu*

Classification C

Subject

References

Author 宋 劉義慶 撰 *Written by Sung, Liu I-Ching*

Edition 葛氏嘯園版 *Ko-Shih, Hsiao-Yuan ed.*

Index

Bound in *1 tao   20 chuan   8 tsè.*

Remarks

380

. . . .

54

Accession No. *1484*   Index No. *149-m h i*

Title 善睡編 *Ching Shui Pien*

Classification *C-328.*

Subject *Extracts of essays from various works with moral teachings.*

References

Author 清華榮萱纂 *Compiled by* *Ching. Hua Jang-Hsüan*

Edition 家藏版 ~~Home Library~~ *Private family edition*

Index *None.*

Bound in *1 tao   4 chuan 8 tsê.*

Remarks

The University of Toronto Chinese Library
. . . .

Accession No.   *44*   1485   Index No. 128-99b3

Title   聖教史畧 *Shêng Chiao Shih Lueh*

Classification   B

Subject

References

Author   清 蕭若琴 譯 *Ching, Hsiao Jo-Sê translated*

Edition   鉛印本 *Type-setting ed.*

      油光紙 *"Yu-Kuang" paper*

Index

Bound in   1 tao 18 chuan 5 tse.

Remarks

382

The University of Toronto Chinese Library

. . . .

106

Accession No.   1486   Index No. 030-ch3a

Title   名賢手札墨蹟 Ming Hsien Shou Tsia Mo Chi

Classification   D 43

Subject   A collection of hand-writing correspondence by Scholars of the Ching Dynasty.

References

Author

Edition   岵瞻堂摹刻 Hu-Chan-Táng
連史紙 "Lien-Shih" paper

Index

Bound in   1 tao   4 tśe

Remarks

383

63

Accession No.   1487   Index No. 149-8jcm

Title   詩韻合璧 Shih Yün Ho Pi

Classification   C

Subject

References

Author   清 楊文璐校補 Collated & Amended by Ching, Yang Wên-Lu

Edition   松隱閣印 Sung-Ying-Ko published
光緒四年印 Dated, Kuang-Hsü "Wu-Ying" 4/1878
粉紙 "Fēn" paper

Index

Bound in   1 tao   5 chuan   5 ts'e.

Remarks

The University of Toronto Chinese Library
. . . .

Accession No. ~~1988~~ 58   Index No. 039-ajdg

Title   孔子集語 Kung Tzŭ Chi Yü

Classification   C

Subject

References

Author   清 孫星衍撰 Written by Ching, Sun Hsing-Yen

Edition   陽湖孫氏本寫刊 Yang-Hu, Sun-Shih Copied block engraving.

Index

Bound in   1 tao   17 Chuan   6 tse.

Remarks

The University of Toronto Chinese Library

. . . .

Accession No. *17* 1489   Index No. 032-lghh

Title 增兩朝御批正續通鑑類纂
Tsêng Liang Chao Yü Pi Chêng Hsü Tûng Chien Lei Tsuan

Classification B

Subject

References

Author 清 馬佳松椿纂 *Compiled by*
Ching, Ma Chia-Sung-Ch'un

Edition 上海和記書莊石印本
Shanghai, Ho-Chi-Shu-Chuang Book Co. Lithographic ed.

Index

Bound in 1 tao 20 chuan 12 tse.

Remarks

386

. . . .

Accession No. *111* *1490*   Index No. *061-Lecz*

Title 惜抱軒文集 *Hsi Pao Hsüan Wên Chi*

Classification *D*

Subject

References

Author 清姚鼐著 *Ching, Yao Nai*

Edition 桐城徐氏刊 *Tung-Chêng, Hsü-Shih published. blok-engraving*

Index

Bound in *1 tao   26 Chuan   6 tsê.*

Remarks

387

The University of Toronto Chinese Library
. . . .

103

Accession No. *1491*   Index No. *198-zzdd*

Title 鹿洲全集 *Lu Chou Chüan Chi*

Classification

Subject

References

Author 清 藍鼎元著 *Ching, Lan Ting-Yüan*

Edition 同文藏版　中箱本 *Tung-Wên privately printed block preserved. Pocket-ed*
同治壬申年刊　毛邊紙
"Mao-Pien" paper

Index *Dated, Tung-Chih "Jên-Shen" 11/1892*

Bound in 4 *tao*　　20 *chüan*　　24 *tsê*

Remarks

388

64

Accession No.   1492   Index No. 042-33h

Title   小豆棚 *Hsiao Tou Pêng*

Classification   C-510   Folk-lore

Subject   a collection of folk-stories from different sources.

References

Author   清曾衍東著 *Ching, Tseng Yen-Tung*

Edition   上海申報館 仿聚珍版印 *Shanghai; Sheng-Pao (Shanghai Newspaper)*

Index   Table of Contents.

Bound in   1 tao   16 chuan   6 tsé.

Remarks

Accession No. 3 1493   Index No. 031-b乃太太

Title 四書偶談 續編 Ssŭ Shu Ou Tán Hsü Pien

Classification A-131. The Four Book

Subject A miscellaneous expository studies on terms + other topics of the Four Books.

References

Author 清 戚翰芳著 Ching, Chi Han-Fang

Edition 家藏版 ~~Home Library~~ private family edition

Index none

Bound in 1 tao 1 tsé

Remarks

68

Accession No.   1494   Index No. 149 - im

Title   諧 鐸   Hsieh To

Classification   C -387   Colloquial Novels.

Subject   a collection y Short stories with
        moral teachings

References

Author   清 沈起鳳著 Ching, Shên Chi-fêng

Edition   上海 鴻寶齋 石印
        Shanghai, Hung-Pao-Chia lithographic ed.

Index   Table y Contents

Bound in   1 tao   12 chuan   4 ts'e.

Remarks

391

The University of Toronto Chinese Library

. . . .

Accession No. 120 1495   Index No. 067-zeeh

Title 文苑英華辨証 Wên Yüan Ying Hua Pien Chêng

Classification D-93 總集一文

Subject

References

Author 宋彭淑夏撰 Written by Sung, Pêng Shu-Hsia

Edition 清武英殿聚珍版印 Ching, Wu-Ying-place Pocket-ed.

Index

Bound in 1 tao 10 chuan 4 tsé.

Remarks

The University of Toronto Chinese Library

. . . .

✓

2

Accession No.   1496   Index No. 198- l g k z

Title   麟經摘珠 Lin Ching ~~chih~~ Chai Chu

Classification   A- 101

Subject   a hand written extracts from
          the Spring & Autumn Annals.

References

Author   胡傳删 Hu Chuan shan.

Edition   抄本 Manuscript copy
          毛邊紙 Mao-pien paper

Index

Bound in   1 tao   2 tsé.

Remarks

. . . .

10

Accession No. *1497*   Index No. *072-d g g e*

Title 易經通註 *I Ching Tung Chu*

Classification A *11*

Subject

References

Author 清傅以漸奉勅撰 *Ching Fu I-Chien ~~Fêng~~ Written*
Old-time - Manuscripts + pocket-sized
Edition 舊精抄巾箱本 原紅格底本 *Original*
龍門紙 夾板 *"Lung-Men" paper   wooden folder*

Index

Bound in 1 *tao* 9 *Chuan* 8 *tsé.*

Remarks

65

Accession No. *1498* Index No. *128- ecc8*

Title 聊齋志異新評 *Liao Chai Chih I Hsin Ping*

Classification *C ~ 368*

Subject

References

Author 清蒲松齡 撰 *Written by Ch'ing, P'u Sung-Ling*

Edition 廣順但氏刊 *Kuang- Shun, Tan-Shih blocks.*
碟批評點本 *Commentaries printed in red*

Index

Bound in *2 tao   16 chuan 16 tsè.*

Remarks

The University of Toronto Chinese Library

. . . .

54

Accession No. 1499   Index No. 120·989n

Title 經策通纂 Ching Tsê Tung Tsuan

Classification C

Subject

References

Author 清 吳澄夫 輯 Compiled by Ching, Wu Chêng Fu

Edition 點石齋石印 Tien-Shih-Chai Lithographic ed.

Index

Bound in 10 Tao   56 Chuan   80 Tsê.

Remarks

396

The University of Toronto Chinese Library

. . . .

67

Accession No. 1500   Index No. 074.2bp8

Title 朝市叢載 Chao Shih Tsung Tsai

Classification C

Subject

References

Author 清楊靜亭原輯 李虹若纂輯
Originally Compiled by Ching, Yang Ching-Ting, Li, Hung-Ju
Edition 文光樓藏版 Wên-Kuang-Lou block preserved edition private printed
光緒年刻 毛太紙
"Mao-Tai" paper
Index   Dated, Kuang-Hsü period (1875-1908)

Bound in 1 tao 8 chuan 8 tsê.

Remarks

The University of Toronto Chinese Library

. . . .

Accession No. *1500*   Index No. *074-2b83*

Title 朝市叢載 *Chao Shih Tsung Tsai*

Classification *C — 348 朝叢志 ?*

Subject *a general information for people to visit the Capital — "Peking"*

References

Author

Edition 京都文光楼藏板
Ching-Tu, Wên-Kuang Lou edition   *blocks preserved*

Index *seperate table of contents for each Chüan*

Bound in *1 t'ao, 8 ts'ê*

Remarks

398

The University of Toronto Chinese Library

. . . .

32

Accession No. _1501_   Index No. _108-9889_

Title 盛京路程 _Shêng Ching Lu Chêng_

Classification β-233 地書

Subject

References

Author

Edition 抄寫本繪圖 _Manuscript with pictures_
白綿紙 _White "Mien" paper_

Index

Bound in 1 tao 2 ts'e.

Remarks

399

The University of Toronto Chinese Library

. . . .

97

Accession No. 1502   Index No. 102-eeka

Title   留節盦尺牘叢殘 Liu Mao An Chih Tu Tsung Tsan

Classification   D⌵-43

Subject

References

Author   清嚴士竹稿 (:) Chíng, Yen Shih Chu (unpublished) draft

Edition   家藏版 Privated- printed edition. family

　　　　 咸豐年刻 毛太紙 "Mao-Tao" paper
　　　　　　　　　　　　 Dated, Hsien-Fēng period 1851-1861

Index   1

Bound in   1 Tao   4 chuan   4 tsé.

Remarks

400

. . . .

73

Accession No. 1503   Index No. 061-ʒ lih

Title 憩影偶錄 Hsi Yin Ou Lu

Classification C 328.

Subject Extracts from various works compiled
under different topics.

References

Author 清張埏輯 Compiled by
Ching, Chang Yen

Edition 南潯書屋藏版 Nan Chi shu Wu block preserved.
嘉慶年刊, 連史紙 Dated, Chia-Ching period 1796-1820
"Nien-Shih" paper

Index

Bound in 1 tao   8 chuan   8 tse.

Remarks

The University of Toronto Chinese Library

. . . .

106

Accession No. *1504*   Index No. *106-azgc*

Title 百大家名賢手札 *Pai Ta Chia Ming Hsien Shou Cha*

Classification *己—53* 農家 *D—43* 別集一文

Subject *A collection of famous letters*

References '

Author 圉

Edition 醉二室西法影印 *Tsui-Erh-Shih-Hsi-Fa Ying published* *Photo-lithographic*
連史紙 *"Nien-shih" paper*
光緒年印 *Dated, Kuang-Hsü period 1875—1908*

Index
none

Bound in *1 tao   6 tse.*

Remarks

402

17

Accession No. *1505*   Index No. *031-↑b3*

Title   國史畧 *Kuo Shih Lüeh*

Classification   *B 227   Foreign Countries*

Subject   *An outline of Japanese history*
in Chinese with Japanese phonics
of a Japanese writer.

References

Author   日本松苗編 *edited by Sung Mao (Japan)*

Edition   日本刻版 *Japanese edition printing*
竹紙 *bamboo paper*
明治戊辰年刻本 *Dated, Ming-Chih "Wu-Chên" 1868 — 1911*

Index

Bound in   *1 tao   8 chuan   2 tsie.*

Remarks

The University of Toronto Chinese Library

. . . .

62

Accession No. 15-06   Index No. 032-lezd

Title 憎定金批 西廂 Tseng Ting Chin Pi Hsi Hsiang

Classification C

Subject

References

Author

Edition ~~Ju-Shih-Shen-Fang edition~~ 如是山房版 殊批評點 Commentaries Printed in Red.
光緒丙子年刻 白紙. White paper
Dated, Kuang-Hsü "Ping-Tzǔ" 2/1816

Index

Bound in 1 tao   6 chuan 6 tsé

Remarks

The University of Toronto Chinese Library

. . . .

66

Accession No. 1507   Index No. 120-cc gg

Title 級齋畫賸 Jen Chai Hua Shêng Fêng

Classification C-223   Calligraphy & Painting

Subject A collection of paintings (woodcut)

References

Author

Edition 陳氏得古歡室精刻本 Chên-shih, Tu-Ku-Huan-Shih, fine-printed
光緒丙子年刻 Dated, Kuang-Hsü "Ping-Tzu" 2/1876

Index

Bound in 1 tao 4 chuan.

Remarks

405

√ x
√ illus.

The University of Toronto Chinese Library
. . . .
22

Accession No. 1508   Index No. 060- 避暑 山
御明园圖

Title 御製 避暑山莊 *Yü Chih* *Pi Shu Shan Chuang*
圓明園圖詠 *Yüan Ming Yüan* *Tu Yüng*

Classification ~~BL 223~~
D-1508

Subject

References *Toronto No. 776,*

Author 清徐氏摹 *Ching, Hsü Shih (copy)*

Edition 大同書局石印本 *Ta-Tung Book Co. Lithographic edition*
綿連紙   *"Mien-Nien" paper*

Index

Bound in 1 *tao*, 2 *ts'e*

Remarks

406

The University of Toronto Chinese Library

....

49

Accession No. _1509_   Index No. _001-bbel_

Title 三元秘授 _San Yüan Pi Shou_

Classification _C-308_

Subject

References

Author 桐城張氏著 _Túng-Ch'êng Chang-Shih_

Edition 百忍堂藏版 _Pai-Jên-Táng Home Library_   _blocks preserved._

毛太紙 _"Mao-Tai" paper_

Index

Bound in _1 tao, 6 chi (集), 6 ts'ê_

Remarks

The University of Toronto Chinese Library

. . . .

124

Accession No. _1510_   Index No. 030-g c p 8

Title 唐代叢書 _Táng Tai Tsúng Shu_

Classification E

Subject

References

Author 清王文誥輯 *Compiled by* Ching, Wang Wên-Kao

Edition 家藏版 ~~Prirated~~ ~~printed~~ Private family edition
白毛太紙 共六集一百六十四種
White "Mao-Tia" paper

Index

Bound in 6 tao, 36 ts'ê

Remarks

408

The University of Toronto Chinese Library

. . . .

Accession No. _80_ _1511_   Index No. _035-ghch_

Title 夏商合傳 _Hsia Shang Ho Chuan_

Classification _B-52_

Subject

References

Author 清鍾惺伯編輯 _edited & compiled by_ _Ching, Chung Hsing-Po_

Edition 稽古堂刊 _Chi-Ko-Tang Published block-engraving._

Index

Bound in _1 tao, 10 chuan, 8 ts'ê_

Remarks

409

. . . .

73

Accession No. *1512*   Index No. *128-33x* *h*

Title 耳食錄 *Ênh Shih Lu*

Classification *C-510*

Subject

References

Author 清樂官譜著 *Ching, Yüeh Kuan-Pu*

Edition 夢花樓藏版 *Mêng-Hua-Lou private-printed* *block preserved.*

乾隆壬子年刻　綿連紙 *"Mien-Lien" paper*

Dated, Chien-Lung "Jên-Tzǔ" 57/1792

Index

Bound in *1 tao, 16 chuan, 6 ts'ê*

Remarks

410

. . . .

22

Accession No. 1513   Index No. 024-gcbg

Title 南北史掆華 *Nan Pei Shih Chün Hua*

Classification B

Subject

References

Author 清周嘉猷著 *Ching, Chou Chia-Yu*

Edition 家藏版 *Private printed family edition.*
白紙 *White paper*

Index

Bound in 1 tao, 8 chuan, 4 ts'ê

Remarks

411

. . . .

64

Accession No. 1514   Index No. 167-dj

Title 鏡花緣 Ching Hua Yüan

Classification C-387 368 C-387

Subject

References

Author 清李汝珍撰 Written by Ching, Li Ju-Chên

Edition 翠筠山房刻版 Ts'ai-Yün-Shan-Fang private-printed
竹紙 bamboo paper

Index

Bound in 2 tao, 16 ts'ê

Remarks

The University of Toronto Chinese Library

. . . .

93

Accession No. 1515   Index No. 140-P320

Title 蘇黃尺牘 Su Huang Chih Tu

Classification D

Subject

References

Author 黃靜御簽輯 *Compiled by* Huang Ching-Yü

Edition 同人堂版 Tung-Jên-Tang edition.
乾隆癸丑年刻 白毛邊紙 White "Mao-Pien" paper
Dated, Chien-Lung "Kuei-Chou" 58/1793

Index

Bound in 1 Tao, 4 chuan, 4 ts'è

Remarks

93

Accession No. 1516   Index No. 102-eeka

Title 留荝盫尺牘叢殘 Liu Mao An Chih Tu Tsúng Tśan

Classification D

Subject

References

Author 清嚴土竹著 Ching, Yen Shih-Chu

Edition 寶書堂版 Pao-Shu-Tóng edition
竹紙 bamboo paper

Index

Bound in 1 tao, 4 chuan, 4 tsʼê

Remarks

414

The University of Toronto Chinese Library

. . . .

73

Accession No. _1517_   Index No. _102-7269_

Title 異談可信錄 I Tan Kó Hsing Lu

Classification C-510

Subject

References

Author 清鄧瑄輯 Ching, Têng Hsüan   Compiled

Edition 碧山樓藏版 Pi-Shan-Lou private-printed blocks preserved.

Index

Bound in 2 tao, 23 chuan, 12 ts'ê

Remarks

The University of Toronto Chinese Library

. . . .

64

Accession No. 1518   Index No. 161-88ic

Title 農桑輯要 Nung Sang Chi Yao

Classification Č-53 農家

Subject Agriculture

References

Author 元司農司撰 Written by Yüan, Ssŭ Nung-Ssu

Edition 倣聚珍版刻本 (Fang-Chü-Chên) Copy from Movable-type ed.
綿連紙 "Mien-Lien" paper

Index A general table of contents for 7 chüan

Bound in 1 Tao, 7 Chuan, 3 ts'ê

Remarks

416

The University of Toronto Chinese Library

．．．．．．．．．．．．．．．．．．．．．．

104

Accession No. 1519   Index No. 166-biseg

Title 重編留青新集 Chúng Pien Liu Ching Hsin Chi

Classification 刀二33

Subject

References

Author 清伊氏重編 Ching, I Shih (re-edited)

Edition 銅鑄版 巾箱本 Rubbing edition, Pocket edition
        光緒戊子年印 洋粉連紙 "Yong-Fên-Lien" paper
        Dated, Kuang-Hsü "Wu-Tzǔ" 14/1888

Index

Bound in 2 Tao, 24 chuan, 12 ts'ê

Remarks

Accession No. 1520   16

Index No. 196·c7丛 n

Title 鳳洲綱鑑會纂 fêng Chou Kang Chien Hui Tsüan

Classification B-22

Subject

References

Author 明王世貞撰 Written by Ming, Wang Shih-Chên

Edition 石印本 Lithographic edition
光緒庚寅上海鴻文書局印附資治通鑑綱目三編四卷二册
綿連紙 夾版 "Mien-Lien" paper Wood-block
Edition — Shanghai, Hung-Wei Book Co.

Index Dated — Kuang-Hsü "Kêng-Ying" 16/1890

Bound in 1 tao, 73 chuan, 16 ts'ê

Remarks

418

The University of Toronto Chinese Library

· ·

124

Accession No. 1521   Index No. 032-lbdh

Title 增訂集錄 Tsêng Ting Chi Lu

Classification 氏 D-73

Subject

References

                    edited & compiled by
Author 清于光華編輯, Ching, Yü Kuang-Hua

Edition 心簡齋本 Hsien-Chien-Ch'ai
       白毛太纸 共五十六種 White "Mao-T'ai" paper
                              All To-gether 56 Kinds

Index

Bound in 2 tao, 12 chuan, 12 ts'ê

Remarks

419

. . . .

73

Accession No. 1522   Index No. 001-a李jɔj

Title 七修類槀 *Chi Hsiu Lei Kao*

Classification C-303

Subject

References

Author 清郎仁寶著 *Ching, Lang Jên-Pao*

Edition 耕烟草堂刊 *Kêng-Gen-Ts'ao-Tǐng* *published* *block engraving*
乾隆年刻 白紙 *White paper*
Dated, Ch'ien-Lung period 1736-1795

Index

Bound in 2 Tao, 51 chuan (續集 7 chuan), 16 ts'ê

Remarks

420

. . . .

Accession No. *1523*   Index No. *031-bfeg*

Title 四書味根錄 *Ssŭ Shu Wei Kên Lu*

Classification *A*

Subject

References

Author 清金秋潭著 *Ching, Chin Chiu-Tán*

Edition 點石齋石印 *Tien-Shih-Chai Lithographic edition*
光緒癸未年印　白綿紙 *White "Mien" paper*
Dated, Kuang-Hsü "Kuei-Wei" 9/1883

Index

Bound in *1 tao, 2 ts'ê.*

Remarks

421

The University of Toronto Chinese Library

. . . .

Accession No. 1524   Index No. 201-838ᵃ

Title 黄山谷尺牘 附山谷題跋   Huang Shan Ku Chih Tu —
             Fu Shan Ku Ti Fu

Classification D — 43 别集一丈

Subject An individual collection of prose

References

Author 宋,黄庭堅撰, Written by Sung, Huang Ting-Chien

Edition 浦江紛欣閣校本, 袖珍本
 Pú-Chiang, Fēn-Hsin-Ko revised edition, pocket edition

Index a general table of content for 題跋 4 chüan
 a general table of content for 尺牘 10 chüan

Bound in 1 t'ao, 6 t'sê. 尺牘 Chih Tu 10 chüan, 4 t'sê ;
          题跋 4 chüan, 2 t'sê.

Remarks Ti Fu

422

The University of Toronto Chinese Library

. . . .

Accession No.   ⁷³ 1525   Index No. 086- l z l c

Title   燕子箋記 Yen Tzu Chien Chi

Classification   D 143 (C ?)

Subject   a libetto on a certain scholar's life story

References

Author   雪韻堂 批點 Hsüeh-Yün-Táng (commentary)

Edition   寄傲山房藏 版 Chi-Ao-Shan-Fang blocks preserved.
同治年刻   竹紙 bamboo paper
                Dated — Tung-Chih period 1862-1874

Index   none, but with list table of contents of every chapter.

Bound in   1 tao   4 tse.

Remarks

423

The University of Toronto Chinese Library

. . . .

21

Accession No. 1526   Index No. 106-dhdh

Title 皇清開國方略 Hwang Ching K'ai Kuo fang liieh

Classification B-22 編年 Pien Nien

Subject The record of the events in the history of the imperial house of the Ching (Manchu) dynasty from A.D. 1583-1644; together with additional matter related to the Manchu dynasty and its origin

References

Author 清 阿桂等奉敕撰 Ching, A Kuei and others Written by order

Edition 上海廣百宋齋校印 Shanghai, Kuang-Pai-Sung-Chai Revised-printing
洋粉連紙 "Yang-Fên-Lien" paper

Index

Bound in 1 Tao, 32 Chuan, 6 Ts'e

Remarks

The University of Toronto Chinese Library

....

4

Accession No. 1527   Index No. 031-6JCg

Title 四書地理攷 Ssŭ Shu Ti Li Kǎo

Classification A—137

Subject

References :

Author 清王亮生著 Ching, Wang Liang-Shêng

Edition 習靜齋刊 Hsi-Ching-Chai published blocks-engraving.
光緒年刻 連史紙 "Lien-Shih" paper
Dated, Kuang-Hsü period 1875-1908

Index

Bound in 1 tao, 15 chuan, 6 ts'ê

Remarks

The University of Toronto Chinese Library

. . . .

64

Accession No. 1528   Index No. 164-スしcg

Title 醉墨軒畫稿 Tsui Mo Hsüan Hua Kao

Classification C-223

Subject

References

Author 清胡郯伯稿 Ching, Hu Tan-Po (draft, unpublished)

Edition 石印本 Lithographic ed.
宣統元年印 綿連紙 "Mien-Lien" paper
Dated. Hsüan-Tüng "Chi-yu" 1/1909

Index

Bound in 1 tao, 4 chuan, 4 ts'ê

Remarks

. . . .

75

Accession No. 1529   Index No. 167-gtg

Title 金剛経 (金剛般若波羅密経) Chin Kang Ching (Chin
                                        Kang Pan go Po Lo Mi Ching)

Classification C-513

Subject

References

Author

Edition Sun-Chung-Lo pocketed.   Manuscript Huang-Shih private ed.
         孫仲樂改袖珍本   寫刻本
         乾隆年刻黄氏藏本   榜紙 "Pang" paper
                          Dated. Chien-Lung period 1936-1820

Index

Bound in 1 tao, 2 ts'e, 2 chuan

Remarks

427

428

The University of Toronto Chinese Library

. . . .

Accession No. 1531   Index No. 075-dhjm

Title 東萊博議 Tung Lai Po I

Classification D — 43 別集一文

Subject an individual collection of prose

References

Written by

Author 宋. 呂祖謙撰 Sung, Lü Tsu-Chien

Edition 以養蓉館藏本, 鉛印 光緒31年 上海寶善齋
印, 洋衫連紙, 圈上注解.
Shuang-Fu-Jung-Kuang edition,
Dated Kuang-Hsü 31/1905. Shanghai Pao-Shan-Chai printed
Western "Fen-Lien" paper

Index a list of works for 4 chüan
a general table of contents for 4 chüan

Bound in 1 t'ao, 4 chüan, 4 ts'ê

Remarks

429

. . . .

49

Accession No. 1532   Index No. 006-gizi

Title 事類統編 Shih Lei Túng Pien

Classification C-348

Subject

References

Author 清黃葆真增輯 Compiled by Ching, Huang Pao-Chen ~~Feng~~ (~~revised~~)

Edition 家藏版 Private-family ~~printed~~ ed

長沙龍氏重校藏版   夾連紙 "Chia-Lien" paper
Ch'ang-Sha, Lung-Shih Second Rivised ed.

Index

Bound in 6 tao, 93 chuan, 36 tsê

Remarks

430

The University of Toronto Chinese Library

. . . .

79

Accession No. 1533   Index No. 118-eagg

Title 第七才子書 (琵琶記) Ti Chi Tsai Tzŭ Shu (Pi Pa Chi)

Classification c-387

Subject

References

Author 清 高則誠 Ching, Kao Tsê-Chêng

Edition 初刊袖珍本 First edition - pocket ed.
雍正乙卯年刊本 綿連紙 "Mien-Lien" paper
Dated, Yung-Chêng "I-Mao" 13/1735

Index

(only one tao on the shelf?)

Bound in 2 tao, 6 chuan, 12 tsê

Remarks

tao no 2.

431

The University of Toronto Chinese Library

. . . .

Accession No. 1534   Index No. 146-3h38

Title 西域聞見錄 Hsi yü wên chien Lu

Classification B-196

Subject

References

Author 長白七十一椿園著 Chang Pai Chi Shih I Chun Yüan

Edition

Index

Bound in 1 Tao, 8 Chuan, 4 冊 tsê

Remarks

432

The University of Toronto Chinese Library

....

Accession No. 64 1535 Index No. 053-98h

Title 庭聞錄 Ting Wên Lu

Classification B-52

Subject

References

Author 清劉健述 given in oral by Ching, Liu Chien

Edition 家藏本 袖珍本 Privat-family ed., Pocket-ed.

綿連紙 "Mien-Lien" paper

Index

Bound in 1 tao, 6 chuan, 4 tsê

Remarks

Accession No. 1536   Index No. 032-l93∠

Title 墨梅小錄 Mo O Hsiao Lu

Classification ℓ — 63 醫家
            C — 218 藝術
Subject   C — 283 草木

References

Author

Edition 學圃山農重校版, 明吳繼壴十一年精刻小篇
乾隆丁亥年鋸, 綿連紙

Hsüeh P'u Shan Nun revised edition Ming, Wu Chi-Shu edition
fine printed, pocket edition, dated Chien-Lung "Ting-Hai" /1767, "Mien Lien" paper.

Index a general table of contents for 6 t'se and
separate table of contents for each t'se

Bound in 1 t'ao, 6 t'se

Remarks

434

The University of Toronto Chinese Library

. . . .

~~127~~

Accession No. 1537   Index No. 149-8m

Title 詩觸 Shih Chu

Classification

Subject

References

Author 清朱琰輯 Compiled by Ching, Chu yen

Edition 家藏版 中箱本 Private- ~~printed~~ family ed., Pocket ed.
共計十六種 土綿連紙 "Tu-Mien-Lien" paper
                      All together 16 kinds

Index

Bound in 2 tao, 5 chuan, 12 tsé

Remarks

435

The University of Toronto Chinese Library

. . . .

21

Accession No.   1538   Index No. 128-glcß

Title 聖廟祀典圖考 附聖蹟圖 *Shêng Miao Ssŭ Tien Tú Káo Fu Shêng Chi Tú*

Classification B-117 傳記一緣錄

Subject — Biographies of Confucians and his disciples & followers; with illustrations; places occupied in the Confucian Temple, & eulogies of various emperors.

References

Author 清顧子沅輯 *Ching, Ku Tzŭ-Yüan* *Compiled by*

Edition 上海同文書局 *Shanghai Tung-Wen Book Co.* 縮印本
       綿連紙 *"Mien-Lien" paper*

Index

Bound in 1 tao, 4 tsê

Remarks

436

106

Accession No. 1539   Index No. 156-9392

Title 趙文敏寫本兩漢策要 Chao Wên Min Hsieh Pên Liang Han
Tsê Yao

Classification

Subject

References

Author 元趙孟頫撰   張朝樂 校 閱 Written by Yüan, Chao Mêng-Fu,
                              Chang Chao-Lo (collated)

Edition 同文書局石印 Tung-Wen Book Co. Lithographic ed.
光緒年刻   連史紙 "Mien-Lien" paper
Dated, Kuang-Hsü period 1875-1908

Index

Bound in 1 Tao, 12 chuan, 8 tsê

Remarks

. . . .

32

Accession No.   1540   Index No. 144-jnlk

Title 衛藏識圖 Wei Tsang Shih Tú

Classification B-177 地理

Subject

References

Author 清馬少雲撰 Written by Ching, Ma Shao-yün

Edition 家藏版 Private-printed family edition
乾隆年刻   粉紙 "Fên" paper
Dated, Ch'ien-Lung period 1736-1795

Index

Bound in 1 Tao. 2 chuan, 4 tsé

Remarks

438

The University of Toronto Chinese Library

. . . .

Accession No. 1541   Index No. 077-lcch

Title 歷代名賢手札 Li Tai Ming Hsien Shou Tsa

Classification D-23 總集一文

Subject a general collection of letters written
by famous authors

References

                              Compiled by
Author 清 蕭李出枏, Ching, Hsiao Chi-Kung

Edition 雪古齋石印, 光緒年印, 粉紙
        Hsüeh-Ku-Chai, lithographic edition
        "Fên" paper ∧ , dated Kuang-Hsü Period (1875-1908)

Index a general table of contents for 8 Chüan

Bound in 1 t/30, 8 Chüan, 8 Hsê

Remarks

439

72

Accession No.　1542　　　　Index No. 042-3c

Title　小嫏嬛仙館類書十二種　Hsiao Lang Huan Hsien Kuan Lei
Shu Shih Êrh Chung

Classification　C-348

Subject

References

Author　小嫏嬛仙館增訂　Hsiao Lang Huan Hsien Kuan amened bound

Edition　羣玉閣彙刻　Chün-Yu-Ko

同治六年刻　　白紙　White paper

Dated, Tung-Chih "Ting-Mao" 6/1867

Index

Bound in　1 tao　22 chuan (十二種)　8 ts'ê

Remarks

The University of Toronto Chinese Library

. . . .

Accession No. 67/1543   Index No. 067-ʒdgl

Title 文林畫譜 Wên Lin Hua Pù

Classification C-223

Subject

References

Author 致芳軒主人寫 Chih Fang Hsüan Chu Jen ~~Hsieh~~ manuscript.

Edition 日本版 Japanese ed.
明治年刻　白紙 White paper
Dated, Ming-Chih period (1868-1911)

Index

Bound in 2 tao, 17 chuan, 17 Ts'ê

Remarks

441

The University of Toronto Chinese Library

. . . .

Accession No. ~~3~~ 1544   Index No. 149-jjdm

Title 詩韻全璧 Shih Yün Chuan Pi

Classification A

Subject

References

Author

Edition 惜陰書室藏版　積山書局石印　blocks preserved　Chi-Shan Book Co. Lithographic ed.
Hsi-Yin-Shu-Shih ~~Private~~ ed.
光緒年印　綿連紙　"Mien-Lien" paper
Dated, Kuang-Hsü period 1875-1908

Index

Bound in 1 tao, 6 ts'ê

Remarks

. . . .

64

Accession No. 1545   Index No. 008-ﾞkﾞﾑ

Title 京塵雜錄 Ching Ch'en Tsa Lu

Classification C

Subject

References

Author 清楊掌生著 Ching, Yang Chang-Shêng

Edition 上海同文書局石印 Shanghai, Tung-Wen Book Co Lithographic ed.

Index

Bound in 1 tao, 4 chuan, 2 ts'ê

Remarks

443

The University of Toronto Chinese Library

. . . .

36

Accession No. 1546   Index No. 072-eccz

Title 昭代名人尺牘小傳 Chao Tai Ming Jen Chih Tu Hsiao Chuan

Classification 丑D-143

Subject

References

Author 清吳修采輯 Compiled by Ching, Wu Hsiu Tsai

Edition 石印版 Lithographic ed.
連史紙 "Lien-Shih" paper

Index

Bound in 1 tao, 24 chuan, 2 ts'ê

Remarks

The University of Toronto Chinese Library

. . . .

45

Accession No. 1547   Index No. 146-3nc

Title 西藏記 Hsi Tsang Chi

Classification B-196

Subject

References

Author

Edition 白紙 White paper

Index

Bound in 1 tao, 2 chuan, 4 ts'ê

Remarks

The University of Toronto Chinese Library

. . . .

Accession No. 1548   Index No. 187-7dc0

Title 駢雅訓纂 *Pien* Ping Ya Hsün Chuan

Classification 七—328 報 4 一 報 纂

Subject Extracts from various works

References

Author 清, 朱沐鍏纂, *Compiled by* Ching, Chu Mou-Wei

Edition 積山書局石印 光緒卅年
Chi-Shan Book Company, dated Kuang-Hsü 30/1904

Index a table of contents for introduction and
a table of contents for 16 chüan

Bound in 1 t'ao, 16 chüan, 8 ts'e

Remarks

446

The University of Toronto Chinese Library

. . . .

Accession No. 114 1549   Index No. 140-0 ecj

Title 藝苑名言 I Yüan Ming Yen

Classification D

Subject

References

Author 清蔣瀾纂輯 Compiled by Chíng, Chiang Lan

Edition 懷古軒藏版 袖珍本 'Pocket ed.
Huai-Kô-Hsien private ed.
乾隆乙未年刊 白紙 White paper
Block-Preserved in Huai Ku Hsüan
Dated, Chʻien-Lung "I-Wei" 40/1775

Index

Bound in 1 tao, 8 chuan, 4 tsʻê

Remarks

447

The University of Toronto Chinese Library

．．．．．．．．．．．．．．．．．．．．．．．．

Accession No. 1550   Index No. 085-l23c

Title (內)泉日記 Chien Chüan Jih Chi

Classification C-308 韓鏢文

Subject miscellaneous writings; with commentary

References

Author 宋韓鏢撰。 Written by Sung, Han Piao

Edition 武英殿聚珍原本 乾隆年刊, 粉紙
Wu-Ying-Tien Chü-chên original copy, dated "Chien-Lung" period (1736-1795), "Fên" paper.

Index a list of the number of works for each chüan

Bound in 1 t'ao, 3 chüan, 3 pên

Remarks

448

The University of Toronto Chinese Library

. . . .

Accession No. *1551*   Index No. *060-hhng*

Title 御製擬白居易新樂府 *Yü Chih Ni Pai Chü I Hsin Yüeh Fu*

Classification *D一43 刘集一文*

Subject *an individual collection of prose*

References

Author *精刻本，同化纸，蓝龙格印*
Fine printed, "Kai-Hua" paper, "Lan Lung-Kö" print
Edition   *edition*

Index *none*

Bound in *1 t'ào, 4 t'iè*

Remarks

449

The University of Toronto Chinese Library

....

Accession No. 1553   Index No. 167-88jc

Title 金川瑣記 chin chuan so chi

Classification C-308 雜史

Subject Miscellaneous writings about 金川; with commentary.

References

Author 清. 李心衡著 ch'ing, Li Hsin-Hêng

Edition 官板. 嘉慶年刻, 竹紙
official printed edition, dated Chia-ching period (1796-1820)
Bamboo paper

Index a general table of contents for 6 chüan

Bound in / t'ao, 6 chüan, 4 ts'e

Remarks

. . . .

Accession No. *119* 1554   Index No. 044-a0id

Title 尺牘新鈔 *Chih Tu Hsin Cháo*

Classification D 73

Subject *a Collection of letters*

References

Author 清 周亮工 輯 *compiled by* *Ching, Chou Liang-Kung*

Edition 海山仙館叢書 *Hai- Shan-Hsien-Kuan* *separate edition from a Collectanea.*
道光年刻. 白紙 *White paper*
Dated, Tao-Kuang period 1821—1850

Index

Bound in 1 *tao* 12 *Chuan* 5 *tse.*

Remarks

451

Accession No. *1555*   Index No. *077-3JP3*

Title 止園叢書 *Chih Yüan Tsung Shu*

Classification *D —* 叢書

Subject

References

Author 清尹昌衡著 *Ch'ing, Yin Ch'ang-Hêng*

Edition

中華書局鉛印, 民國七年印, 連史紙
Chung Hua Shu Chü type-setting edition, dated Republic 7/1918.
"Lien-Shih" paper

Index *A general table of content for* 止園易銖全冊
"Chich Yüan I Shu Ch'üan Tsê"

Bound in 9 *Chung*, 13 *Tsê*

Remarks

The University of Toronto Chinese Library
. . . .

Accession No. 1556   Index No. 085- zhkkl

Title 水滸圖贊 Shui Hu Tu Tsan

Classification 乙—223 藝術—書畫

Subject Calligraphy and painting of "水滸傳"

References

Author 明. 杜堇 繪 Written by Ming. Tu Chin

Edition 羊城廣百宋齋藏版. 綿連紙
Yang-Chêng Kuang-Pai Sung-Chai Preserved edition, "Mien-Lien" paper

Index a list of names of the pictures for 2 tse

Bound in 1 t'ao. 2 tsê

Remarks

453

Accession No. *129*   *1557*   Index No. *085·ㄥdㄊe*

Title 涵芬樓秘笈 *Han, Fên Lou Pi Chi*

Classification *圭C-338*

Subject

References

Author 涵芬樓輯 *Compiled by Han-Fên-Lou*

Edition 影印本 *Photo-Lithographic ed.*
共五集二十七種 連史紙 *"Lien-Shih" paper*
                          All together 27 kinds

Index

Bound in 5 tao, 40 ts'ê

Remarks

37

Accession No. _1559_   Index No. _039/mbhn_

Title 學古堂藏書目 Hsiao Ku Tang Tsang Shu Mu

Classification

Subject

References

Author 清黃捐藏 Chiang, Huang Chüan preserved. 羅田周氏藏竹紙

Edition 家藏版 Private family Home Edition

Bamboo paper.

Index

Bound in 4 chuan 1 tse

Remarks

The University of Toronto Chinese Library

. . . .

Accession No. ¹⁷ 1560   Index No. 076-Lebg
                                          167-

Title 欽定四庫全書簡明目錄 Chin Ting Ssŭ Ku Chhan Shu
                                          Chien Ming Mu Lu

Classification B-342

Subject

References

Author 清紀昀等奉敕撰 Written by
                      Ch'ing, Chi Chün and others

Edition 廣東書局重刊本 Kuang-Tung Book Co Second ed.
         綿連紙　同治戊辰年刊 "Mien-Lien" paper
         Dated, Tung-Chih "Wu-Chen" 7/1868

Index

Bound in 1 Tao, 20 Chuan, 10 ts'ê

Remarks

Accession No.   1561   Index No. 032-lekh

Title 增定漢魏六朝別解 Tsêng Ting Han Wei Liu Chʻao Pieh Chieh

Classification C-328

Subject

References

Author 明葉紹秦纂 Compiled by Ming, Yeh Shao-Chin

Edition 明崇禎版 Ming, Chʻung-Chên period 1628-1643

Index

Bound in 2 tao, 62 chuan, 24 tsʻê

Remarks

The University of Toronto Chinese Library

. . . .

Accession No.   70   1562   Index No. 140-93m3

Title 莊子獨見 Chuang Tzǔ Tu Chien

Classification C-731

Subject

References

Author 清胡文英評釋 Ch'ing, Hu Wên-Ying (commentaries and annotations)

Edition 家藏版 Private-printed family edition
乾隆年刻 毛太紙 "Mao-Tai" paper
Dated, Ch'ien-Lung period 1736-1795

Index

Bound in 1 tao, 33 chuan, 4 ts'ê

Remarks

The University of Toronto Chinese Library

. . . .

Accession No. 1563   Index No. 044-dih

Title 居業錄 Chü Yeh Lu

Classification C—731 匠吾

Subject Taoism

References

Author 明, 胡居仁 著, 張宇玉 備校
Ming, Chü Hu Chü-jên, Chang Yu Yü revised

Edition 思補堂藏明刻本 乾隆年刻, 毛邊紙
Ssǔ-Pu-Tang edition, dated: Chien-Lung period (1736-1795)
"Mao-Pien" paper

Index

Bound in 1 tʻao, 8 Chüan, 4 tʻsê

Remarks

459

The University of Toronto Chinese Library

. . . .

Accession No. 1564   Index No. 203 - ejkl
                                             170 - kdzl

Title 垒韻樓遺集   Tai Yün Lou I Chi
      陳孝女遺集 合刻   Chén Hsiao Nü I Chi   Ho Kó

Classification D—33—别集—等文

Subject an individual collection of prose and poetry.

References

Author 青,陳薛杏圭, 陳俶室芳 Ch'ing, Chén Hsüeh Hsin-Yü
                                    and Chén Shu-I

Edition 家藏版, 連史紙
         Private-family edition, "Lien-Shih" paper

Index Seperate table of contents for each kind of writing

Bound in 1 t'ao, 5 kind, 12 chüan, 6 ts'e

Remarks

. . . .

Accession No.　1565　　　　Index No. 011-7229

Title　兩漢刊誤 Liang Han Kán Wu

Classification　B 52

Subject　a historical writing

References

Author　宋 吳仁傑 撰 Written by Sung, Wu Jen Chieh

Edition　金陵書局 刊本 Chin-Ling Book co. published
毛邊紙 "Mao-Pien" paper
同治戊辰年刻 Dated Tung-Chih "Wu-Chén" 7/1868

Index

Bound in　1 tao　10 chuan 2 tse.

Remarks

461

The University of Toronto Chinese Library

....

71

Accession No. 1566   Index No. 125-33 i l
                                      140-g z q h
                                      018-d z d z

Title 老子道德真經   Hsiao Tzŭ Tao Tê Chen Ching
       莊子南華經   Chuang Tzŭ Nan Hua Ching
       列子沖虛真經   Lieh Tzŭ Chúng Hsü Chen Ching

Classification C-731 道家

Subject

Taoism

References

Author 李耳   Li Ênh
        莊周   Chuang Chou
        列禦寇 Lieh Yü Kóu

Edition 明精刻本 石朱批評點 Ming Dynastia Fine-printed
         綿連紙 "Mien-Lien" paper Commentaries Printed in Red

Index   a general table of content for 2 táé

Bound in 2 Tao, 16 ts'ê

Remarks

The University of Toronto Chinese Library

. . . .

60

Accession No. 1567   Index No. 075-dk03

Title 東塾讀書記 Tung Shu Tu Shu Chi

Classification C-13 儒家

Subject Miscellaneous writing about classics and philosophy

References

Author 清陳澧撰, written by Ch'ing, Ch'ên Li

Edition 家藏版 Private - printed family edition
竹紙 Bamboo paper

Index A general table of contents for 25 chüan

Bound in 1 tao, 25 卷 Chüan, 5 ts'ê

Remarks

Accession No. 28 *1568*   Index No. *137-ezbc*

Title 船山公年譜 *Chúan Shan Kung Nien Pu*

Classification B-117 傳記一總錄

Subject *collected biographies*

References

Author 清王之春輯 *Compiled by* *ching, Wang Chih-Chun*

Edition 家藏版 *Private-printed family edition*
綿連紙 *"Mien-Lien" paper*

Index *none*

Bound in *1 tao, 2 tsè* (前後編)

Remarks

464

Accession No. 69 1569   Index No. 146-3.hhc

Title 西清箚記 (并附) Hsi Ching Cha Chi (Ping Fu)

Classification C-223

Subject

References

Author 清 胡敬 輯。 Compiled by Ching, Hu ching

Edition 進呈本 Presented to the (throne).
嘉慶年刻 綿連紙 "Mien-Lien" paper
四卷 附南薰殿圖像二卷, 國朝院畫錄二卷
4 chüan, — "Nan-Hsün" palace pictures 2 chüan
"Kao-Chao-Yuen" index of picture 2 chüan

Index Dated — Chia-Ching period 1796—1820

Bound in 1 tao, 4 ts'e

Remarks

The University of Toronto Chinese Library

. . . .

80

Accession No. 15-70   Index No. 075-az

Title 札逢   Tsa I
              ~~Cha~~ I

Classification C -13 儒家

Subject

References

Author 清孫詒讓撰 *Written by* Ching, Sun I-Jang

Edition 家藏版 *Private-printed family edition*
        光緒�廿年刊 綿連紙 "Mien-Lien" paper
        Dated — Kuang-Hsü "Chia-Wu" 20/1894

Index

Bound in 1 tao, 12 chuan, 4 tsê

Remarks

466

· ·

Accession No. *1571*   Index No. *123-999ᵉ*

Title 羣經義証 *chün Ching I chêng*

Classification *A—137*

Subject

References

Author

Edition *Li-Tu revised ed. Private-printed family edition*
李渡校. 家藏版
連史紙 *"Lien-Shih" paper*

Index

Bound in *1 tao, 8 chuan, 2 tsê*

Remarks

467

. . . .

Accession No. *25* 1572   Index No. 115-jbh

Title 稽古錄 Chi Ku Lu

Classification B -12 正史

Subject official history

References

Author 宋司馬光撰 Written by Sung, Ssŭ Mar-Kuang

Edition 清初刻本 First ed in Ching Dynastie 1644—1911
毛邊紙 "Mao-Pien" paper

Index a general table of contents for 20 chüan

Bound in 1 tao. 20 chüan, 2 tsê

Remarks

468

IX

✓

The University of Toronto Chinese Library

· ·

120

✓ Accession No.   1573   Index No. 120-032

Title 續文選 Hsü Wên Hsüan

Classification D

Subject

References

Author 明胡震亨輯 Compiled by Ming, Hu Chen-Hêng

Edition 明精刻本 Ming Dynastic 1368 — 1643 Find-printed
竹紙 Bamboo paper

Index

Bound in 1 tao, 14 chuan, 8 tsê

Remarks

469

The University of Toronto Chinese Library

. . . .

36

Accession No. 1574   Index No. 076-Lebb

Title 欽定古今儲貳金鑑 *Chin Ting Ku Chin Chin Ênh Chin Chien*

Classification B-107 獨錄

Subject

References

Author 清乾隆帝欽定 *Ching. Chien-Lung* ~~帝~~ *Chin Ting* Emperor

Edition 官版 *Official edition*
毛邊紙 *"Mao-Pien" paper*

Index

Bound in 1 *tao.* 6 *chuan.* 4 *tsê*

Remarks

The University of Toronto Chinese Library

. . . .

Accession No. 7 1575   Index No. 042-363

Title 小四書 Hsiao Ssǔ Shu

Classification 書 e-13

Subject

References

Author 明方逢辰撰 Written by Ming, Fang Pêng-chen

Edition 明嘉靖二十六年刊本 大字精刻 Fine-printed in big letters character ed.
明綿紙 Ming, "Mien" paper
Dated — Ming, Chia-Chin "Ting-Wei" 26/1574

Index

Bound in 1 tao, 5 chuan, 3 tsê

Remarks

. . . .

15

Accession No. *1576*   Index No. *085-3262*

Title 洪憲元年曆書 *Hung Hsien Yüan Nien Li Shu*

Classification 史 C-133

Subject

References

Author 教育部中央觀象台 ~~Chiao Yü Pu~~ *Chung-Yang-Kuang-Hsiang Tai*
                                    of Ministry of Education

Edition 觀象台製 *Kuang-Hsiang-Tai printed*
        白綿紙 *White "Mien" paper*

Index

Bound in *1 tao, 1 tsê*

Remarks

The University of Toronto Chinese Library

....

22

Accession No. 1577   Index No. 167. ze Li

Title 金陀粹編 Chin Tó Sui Pien

Classification B 147

Subject A history on Ching (金) tribe especially her relation with the Sung Emperors.

References

Author 清 岳珂編, edited by Ching, Yüeh Chi

Edition 浙江書局刊 Chê-chiang Book Co. published 光绪癸年刊毛边纸 "Mao-Pien" paper Dated — Kuang-Hsü "Kuei-Wei" 9/1883

Index

Bound in 1 tao 28 chuan 6 tse

Remarks

The University of Toronto Chinese Library

. . . .

62

Accession No.   1578   Index No. 001-dging

Title 世說新語 Shih Shuo Hsin Yü

Classification C-368

Subject

References

Author 宋劉義慶撰 Written by Sang, Liu I-Ching

Edition 明凌濛初訂版 Ming, Ling-Mêng first ed.
竹紙 Bamboo paper

Index

Bound in 1 tao, 1 chuan (附補註) 5 tsê

Remarks

. . . .

113

Accession No.   1579   Index No. 085-igd

Title 測海集 Tsê Hai Chi

Classification D-23

Subject

References

Author 清彭紹升著 Ching, Pêng Shao-Shêng

Edition 寶翰樓藏版 "Pao-Han-Lou Private printed block-preserved ed.
貴州綿紙 Kuei-Chou "Mien" paper

Index

Bound in 1 tao, 6 chuan, 4 tsê

Remarks

475

46
古

Accession No. 1J-80 ?   Index No. 030/ b b l f

Title   古今偽書致   Ku Ching Wei Shu Kao

Classification

Subject

References

Author

Edition   清姚首原著 Ching, Yao Shan, 毛太紙 Mao Tai paper
          浙江書局版 cheking press
          光緒十八年刻 Kuang Hsü (18th year)

Index

Bound in   two Chuan

Remarks

476

The University of Toronto Chinese Library

. . . .

80

Accession No.　　1581　　　　Index No. 167-3jcc

Title　金谿順齋先生策海 Chin Chi Shun Chai Hsien Shêng Tsê Hai

Classification　C-308 雜家一雜文

Subject

References

Author　明張順齋撰　門人沈季文編次　Written by Ming, Chang Shun Chai

Edition　白紙　White paper　　　Shên Chi-Wên (revised)

明刻本 Ming Dynastie 1368-1643

Index　a general index of the references

　　　　a general table of content for 22 chuan

Bound in　1 tao,　22 chuan,　12 tsê

Remarks

. . . .

93

Accession No.   *1582*   Index No. *075-mhhd*

Title   楳華館全集 *Chêng Hua Kuan Chuan Chi*

Classification *D-23*

Subject

References

Author   清路德著 *Ching, Lu Tê*

Edition   家藏版 *Private-printed family edition*
光緒七年閣迺竹校刊 綿連紙 *"Mien-Lien" paper*
Dated— Kuang-Hsü "Hsing-Ssü" 7/1881

Index

Bound in *1 tao, 12 chuan, 10 tsê*

Remarks

11

Accession No. 1J-83   Index No. 030-bae8

Title 古本尚書 *Ku Pêng Shang Shu*

Classification A

Subject

References

Annotated by
Author 元金治仁山表註 *Yüan, Chin Jen-Shan Piao*

Edition 掃葉山房映寫原本刊 *Sao-Yeh-Shan-Fang*
光緒年刊 綿連紙 "Mien-Lien" paper
Dated — *Kuang-Hsü period 1825—1908*

Index

Bound in 1 *tao*, 2 *tsa* (上下)

Remarks

479

The University of Toronto Chinese Library

. . . .

28

Accession No.   1584   Index No. 115-e0c?

Title   秦邊紀略 Chin Pien Chi Lüeh

Classification B

Subject

References

Author

Edition   半畝園藏書本 Pan-Mou-Yuan Home-Library
           綿連紙 "Mien-Lien" paper

Index

Bound in 1 tao, 6 chuan, 2 tsê

Remarks

480

The University of Toronto Chinese Library

. . . .

Accession No. 7 1586   Index No. 030-6071

Title 古籀拾遺 Ku Chou Shih I

Classification A

Subject

References

Author 清孫詒讓記 Ching, Sun I-jang

Edition 永嘉戴鍾甍刻本 Yung-Chia, Tai-Chung-Yu
竹紙 Bamboo paper

Index

Bound in 1 tao, 2 chuan, 2 tsê

Remarks

The University of Toronto Chinese Library
....

102

Accession No. 1587   Index No. 061-d7b3

Title 忠宣公文集 Chung Hsüan Kung Wên Chi

Classification D-43

Subject

References

Author 元余闕著 Yüan, Yü Chüeh

Edition 清皖江棗署本 Ching, Huan-Chiang local official ed.
同治丁卯年刊   綿連紙 "Mien-Lien" paper
Dated — Tung-Chih "Ting-Mao" 6/1867

Index

Bound in 1 tao, 6 chuan, 2 tsê

Remarks

25

Accession No. *1588*   Index No. *030-63*

Title 史略 *Shih Lüeh*

Classification *B*

Subject

References

Author 宋高似孫續古 *Sung, Kao Ssü-Sun*

Edition 虞山鮑氏刊本 *Yu-Shan, Pao-Shih published.*
光緒癸未年刻　綿連紙 *"Mien-Lien"paper*
Dated — Kuang-Hsü "Kuei-Wei" 9/1883

Index

Bound in

Remarks

The University of Toronto Chinese Library

．．．．．．．．．．．．．．．．．．．．．．．．

Accession No. 1589   Index No. 154-Lecb

Title 賞奇軒四科合編 & Shang Chi Hsüan Ssŭ Chung Ho Pien

Classification C—223 藝術—書畫

Subject a general collection of galla calligraphy and painting. with commentary

References

Author

Edition 粉印本 "Fên" paper

文德堂藏板 blocks preserved in Wên Tê Tang

Index a table of contents for the first t'se

Bound in 1 t'ao, 4 t'se

Remarks

484

The University of Toronto Chinese Library

....

6

Accession No. _1590_   Index No. _031-b79e_

Title 四書説苑 _Ssŭ Shu Shuo Yüan_

Classification _A_

Subject

References

Author 清孫應科輯 Compiled by _Ch'ing, Sun Ying-Ko_

Edition 家藏版 _Private-printed family edition_
毛邊紙 _"Mao-Pien" paper_

Index

Bound in _1 tao, 11 chuan, 4 tsê_

Remarks

The University of Toronto Chinese Library

. . . .

15

Accession No. *1592*   Index No. *030-638*

Title 古方略 *Ku Fang Lüeh*

Classification *B*

Subject

References

Author 明張自烈述 _{Given in oral by} *Ming, Chang Tzŭ-Lieh*

Edition 忠貞堂版 *Chung-Chen-Tang private ed.*
白蘭言藏書　竹紙 *Pai-Nan-Yen Home-Library*
Bamboo paper

Index

Bound in *2 tao, 51 chuan, 36 tsê*
　　　　3 套,
Remarks

The University of Toronto Chinese Library

. . . .

114

Accession No.   1593   Index No. 149-79

Title   詩説 Shih Shuo

Classification A-31 9

Subject

References

Author 清惠周楊著 Ching, Hui Chou-Ti

Edition 眞意堂刊本 Chên-I-Tâng published
         嘉慶壬申年刊 竹紙 Bamboo paper.
         Dated — Chia-Ching "Jên-Shen" 17/1812
Index

Bound in 1 tao, 3 chuan, 1 tsê

Remarks

The University of Toronto Chinese Library
. . . .

III

✓ <u>Accession No.</u>   *1594*   <u>Index No.</u> *030-bble*

<u>Title</u> 古今辭命達 *Ku Chin Tzŭ Ming Ta*

<u>Classification</u> *D*

<u>Subject</u>

<u>References</u>

<u>Author</u> 明胡正心纂輯   范文燕訂定∧ *Compiled by Ming, Hu Chêng-Hsin, Fan Wên-Yen (revised)*

<u>Edition</u> 明刻本   十竹齋藏版 *Shih-Chu-Chai private-printed*
竹紙   *Bamboo paper*
Dated, Ming Dynastie 1368 — 1643

<u>Index</u>

<u>Bound in</u> *1 tao, 6 chuan, 4 tsʻ*

<u>Remarks</u>

· ·

103

Accession No. 1595   Index No. 085-1933

Title 渠亭山人半部稿 *Chü Ting Shan Jen Pan Pu Kao*

Classification D

Subject

References

Author 清 張貞撰 Written by *Ching, Chang Chên*

Edition 家藏版 *Private-printed family edition*
毛邊紙 *"Mao-Pien" paper*

Index

Bound in 1 *tao.* 8 *tsê* (四種) *Four Kinds*

Remarks

489

The University of Toronto Chinese Library

. . . .

Accession No. 87 1596   Index No. 054-3273c

Title 建國詮真 *Chien Kuo Chüan Chên*

Classification C - 308 雜文

Subject miscellaneous writings about how to build up the country

References

Author 徐樹錚撰 Written by *Hsü Shu-Chêng*

Edition 影印原寫本 Photo-Lithographic from the original manuscripts 綿連紙 "Mien-Lien" paper

Index none

Bound in 1 tao. 4 tsê

Remarks

The University of Toronto Chinese Library

....

Accession No. 87 1597   Index No. 140-讠弓九

Title 萬緣金剛經集註 *Wan Yüan Chin Kang Ching Chi Chu*

Classification C

Subject

References

Author 清增德集註 *Annotated by* *Ching, Tsêng Tê* 4

Edition 家藏版 *Privated-printed family edition*
綿連紙 *"Mien-Lien" paper*

Index

Bound in 1 *tao*, 1 *tsê*

Remarks

491

The University of Toronto Chinese Library

. . . .

97

Accession No. 1598   Index No. 018-bc37

Title 刈存詩草 I Tsun Shih Tsáo

Classification D-38 别集-詩

Subject An individual collection of poetry

References

Author 清劉玉衡著 Chíng, Liu Yü-Hêng

Edition 家藏版 Private-printed family edition
竹紙 Bamboo paper

Index none

Bound in 1 tao 2 tsǒ (上下)

Remarks

492

(p.86)

Accession No. 1599   Index No. 012-乙d3

Title 兼明書 Chien Ming Shu

Classification C-308 雜文

Subject Miscellaneous writings; with commentary

References

Author 唐邱光庭撰 Written by Tang, Chiu Kuang-Ting

Edition 横川吳氏刊 Hêng-Chuan Wu-Shih published
嘉慶年刻 飛清閣藏 毛邊紙 Fei-Ching-Ko private ed. "Mao-Pien" paper
Dated — Chia-Ching period 1796—1820

Index a general table of contents for 5 chuan

Bound in 1 tao, 5 chuan, 4 ts'ê

Remarks

493

The University of Toronto Chinese Library

· ·

(97)

Accession No. 1600   Index No. 067-3eeh

Title 文苑英華選 Wên Yüan Ying Hua Hsüan

Classification D-

Subject

References

Author 官定山輯 Compiled by Kuan Ting-Shan

Edition 光明正大之堂藏版 Kuang-Ming-Chêng-Ta-Chih-Tang
毛邊紙 "Mao-Pien" paper   private printed
block-preserved

Index

Bound in 2 tao, 60 chuan, 24 tsê

Remarks

494

The University of Toronto Chinese Library

. . . .

75-

Accession No. 1601   Index No. 162-ddza

Title 近世一百名家畫集 Chin Shih I Pai Ming Chia Hua Chi

Classification c-223

Subject

References

Author 振青書畫社輯 Chên-Ching-Shu-Hua-Shê Compiled by
Edition 珂羅版影印 民國三年 Kô-Ho Photo-lithographic ed of Kô-Lo ed.
連印紙 "Lien-Ying" paper
Dated, Ming-Kuo 3 Nien 1914

Index

Bound in / Tao, 4 tsê.

Remarks

78

Accession No. 1602   Index No. 149-09cd

Title 讀畫軒印存 *Tu Hua Hsüan Yin Tsun*

Classification C

Subject

References

Author 清王俊集印 *Ching, Wang Chün printed.*

Edition 琴圃藏版 *Ching-Pu private-printed block preserved ed.*
光緒年刻 綿連紙 *"Mien-Lien" paper*
Dated, Kuang-Hsü period (1875-1908)

Index

Bound in 1 Tao, 2 Tsê

Remarks

126

Accession No. *1603*   Index No. *023-iiibi*

Title 區種五種 *Chü Chung Wu Chung*

Classification *X e-53*

Subject

References

Author 清 趙夢齡 輯 *Compiled by* *Ching, Chao Mêng-Ling*

Edition 蓮花池刊 *Lien-Hua-Chih published block-engraving.*

光緒戊寅年刊本 毛邊紙 *"Mao-Pien" paper*

Dated, Kuang-Hsü "Wu-Ying" 4/1878

Index

Bound in *1 tao, 2 tsê*

Remarks

497

The University of Toronto Chinese Library

....

Accession No. /603   Index No. 023-ii bi

Title 芻種芧種 Chü Chung Wu Chung

Classification 農 - 農

Subject Miscellaneous writings of agriculture.

References

Author 清，趙夢齡輯 ~ Ching, Chao Mêng-Ling *compiled by*

Edition 蓮花池刊 光緒戊寅年刊本，毛邊本
Lien-Hua-Chih edition, dated Kuang-Hu-Hsü Period "Wu-Yin" / 1878
"Mao-Pien" paper

Index ~~none~~ a general table of contents for 2 the

Bound in 1 táo, 2 tsê

Remarks

general

The University of Toronto Chinese Library

. . . .

Accession No. 1604   Index No. 077-b3cb

Title 此木軒四書說 Tzǔ Mu Hsüan Ssǔ Shu Shuo

Classification A — 131 四書

Subject a general writing of the Four Books

                general

References

Author 清, 焦袁熹著 Chíng, Chiao Yüan-Hsi

Edition 毛邊版, 清翰林院藏車 毛巴片
Private family home edition, Ching Han-Lin-Yüan preserved edition, "Mao-Pien" paper

Index a list of works for 9 chüan

Bound in 1 t'ao, 9 chüan, 4 ts'ê

Remarks

The University of Toronto Chinese Library

. . . .

61

Accession No. 1605   Index No. 117-iJgb

Title 端溪硯史 Tuan Chi Yen Shih

Classification C

Subject

References

Author 清吳蘭修撰. *Written by* Ching Wu Lan-Hsiu
        Nan-Hai Wu-Shih, Yüeh-Ya-Tang revised ed.

Edition 南海伍氏粵雅堂校刊 精刻本 Fine-Printed edition.
         道光三十年刊 綿連紙 "Mien-Lien" paper
         庚戌
                Dated, Tao-Kuang "Kêng-Hsü" 30/1850

Index

Bound in 1 Tao, 3 chuan, 2 tsê

Remarks

500

The University of Toronto Chinese Library

. . . .

26

Accession No. 1606   Index No. 163-99c3

Title 邵亭知見傳本書目 Lü Ting Chih Chien Chuan Pên Shu Mu

Classification B

Subject

References

Author 清莫友芝撰 written by Ching, Mo Yu-chih

Edition 上海掃葉山房印本 Shanghai, Sao-Yeh-Shan-Fang ed.
民國十七年印 綿連紙 "Mien-Lien" paper
Dated, Ming-Kuo 17 Nien 1928

Index

Bound in 1 tao, 16 chuan, 6 tsë

Remarks

The University of Toronto Chinese Library

. . . .

80

Accession No. 1607   Index No. 128-gmkh

Title 聖學總論 Shêng Hsüeh Tsung Lun

Classification c

Subject

References

Author 清陸肯吉等述 given in oral by Ching, Lu Yü-Chi and others

Edition 古田凝道齋存版 Ku-Dien-Ning-Tao-Chai Preserved edition. 竹紙 bamboo paper

Index

Bound in 1 tao, 8 tsê

Remarks

The University of Toronto Chinese Library

· ·

28

Accession No. 1608   Index No. 030-bb ㄥㄥ

Title 古今賢女傳 Ku Chin Hsien Nü Chuan

Classification B

Subject

References

Author 息園外史 Hsi Yüan Wai Shih

Edition 精印圖畫 Fine-printed picture
綿連紙 "Mien-Lien" paper
no text almost all illus.

Index

Bound in 1 tao, 8 tsê

Remarks

Accession No. 1609 22

Index No. 181-ldgd
169-ẓẓdd

Title 顧林亭先生年譜 Ku Lin Ting Hsien Shêng Nien Pu
閻潛丘先生年譜 Yen Chén Chiu Hsien Shêng Nien Pu

Classification B-107

Subject

References

Author 清 張穆訂 Ching, Chang Mu

Edition 山西壽陽祁氏刊本 Shan-Hsi, Shou-Yang Chi-shih printed ed.
道光二十四年刊 甲辰 綿連紙 "Mien-Lien" paper
Dated, Tao-Kuang "Chia-Chên"
24/1844

Index

Bound in 1 t'ao 2 ts'e

Remarks

504

The University of Toronto Chinese Library

....

1 00

Accession No. 1610   Index No. 030/d 3 3 g

Title 吳氏一家稿 Wu Shih I Chia Kao

Classification

Subject

References

Author 清,吳錫麟等著 Ching, Wu Hsi Ling   連史紙
                                                Lien Shih paper
                        private family
Edition 家藏版 Home edition

咸豐五年刻 Hsien Feng 5th year)

Index

Bound in 16 tie

Remarks

28

Accession No. /611   Index No. 085/ P m c f

Title 瀛環志略 Ying Huan Chih Lueh

Classification B 227

Subject

References

Author 清徐繼畬輯著. *Compiled by* Ching, Hsü Chi-yü

Edition 總理衙門藏版 Chung Li Ya Men *block preserved edition*

同治丙寅年重訂   綿連紙
Dated— Tung Chih Ping Yin   "Mien - Lien" paper.

Index

Bound in 10 Chuan 6 tsê

Remarks

506

The University of Toronto Chinese Library

....

106

Accession No. *1612*   Index No. *073/bcd*

Title 曲江集 *Chü Chiang Chi*

Classification

Subject

References

Author 唐, 張九齡 *Tang, Chang chiu Ling*

Edition 家藏版 ~~Home~~ *private family* Edition
         光緒年刻 *Dated - Kuang Hsü*

Index

Bound in *12 Chuan 8 tse*

Remarks

The University of Toronto Chinese Library
. . . .

103

Accession No. 1613   Index No. 085-Lc 3d

Title 清代人物論 Ching Tai Jen Wu Lun

Classification B-117

Subject

References

Author 清 費有容撰 *Written by* Ching, Fei Yu-jung

Edition 上海廣益書局 石印本 Shanghai, Yuan-I Book Co Lithographic ed.
洋粉連紙 "Yang-Fen-lien" paper

Index

Bound in 1 t'ao   6 ts'ë   14 chuan

Remarks

The University of Toronto Chinese Library

. . . .

Accession No. 1614   Index No. 102-2lh

Title 嘉德錄 Hsü Tê Lu

Classification C－308 輯善－輯錄

Subject miscellaneous writings of the philosophy of
building up good personality.

References

Author 清，席啟圖纂輯 Compiled by Ch'ing. Hsi Chi-Tú

Edition 上海 掃葉山房 石印本，綿連紙
Shanghai, Sao-Yeh Shan-Fang lithographic edition.
"Mien-Lien" paper

Index a general table of contents for 20 Chüan

Bound in 1 t'ao, 20 chüan, 1 ts'ê

Remarks

The University of Toronto Chinese Library

....

Accession No. *1616*   Index No. *167-nl*

Title 鑑撮 四卷附讀史論略一卷
       Chien Ts'o Shih Ssu *chüan Fu Tu Shih Lun Lüeh I chüan*

Classification *3-367*

Subject

References *Toronto No. 1946*

Author 清 曠敏本編。 *edited by Ching, Kuang Min-Pên*

Edition 同治年刊 *Dated, Tung-Chih period (1862→1874)*

Index

Bound in *1 t'ao 5 ts'ê*

Remarks

Accession No. 1617   Index No. 001-66fl
                                      170-ehbf

Title 三史拾遺 附諸史拾遺 San shih shih I
                                Fu Chu shih shih I

Classification B-137

Subject

References

Author 清 錢大昕著 Ch'ing, Chien Ta-Hsin

Edition 嘉興郡版 Chia-Hsing local official edition
        嘉慶十二年刻 連史紙 "Nien-Shih" paper
        丁卯   Dated, Chia-Ching "Ting-Mao" 12/1807

Index

Bound in 1 tao 4 ts'e

Remarks

The University of Toronto Chinese Library

. . . .

13

Accession No. 1619   Index No. 072-edb3

Title 春秋公羊穀梁傳 Chun Chin Kung Yang Ku Liang Chuan

Classification A-101

Subject

References

Author 漢何休學   晉范寗集解 Han, Ho Hsiu-Hsüeh,
                                    Chin, Fan Ning
Edition 金陵書局重刊 Chin-Ling Book Co. Second ed.
         光緒二十年刻 毛邊紙 "Mao-Pien" paper
                      Dated, Kuang-Hsü "Chia-Wu" 20/1894

Index

Bound in 1 t'ao   14 chuan (二種共十四卷) 4 ts'e

Remarks

512

The University of Toronto Chinese Library

....

Accession No. *1621*   Index No. *171-133c*

Title 隸書大字典 *Li Shu Ta Tzŭ Tien*

Classification *B-347*

Subject

References

Author 清 翟云升編（道光十五年）*edited by Ching, Chai Chai Yün-Shêng*

Edition 民國十三年 掃葉山房影印 *Sao-Yeh-Shan-Fang Photo-lithographical Dated, Ming-Kuo 13 Nien 1924*

Index

Bound in *4 Hao 20 ts'ê*

Remarks

Accession No. 31/622   Index No. 030-bcdg

Title 史記鈔, 前漢書鈔, 後漢書鈔 *Shih Chi Chao, Chien Han Shu Chao, Hou Han Shu Chao*

Classification B-12

Subject

References

Author 清 高塘鈔 *Ching, Kao Tang*

Edition 乾隆五十三年 戊申 刊本 *Dated, Ch'ien-Kung "Wu-Chia" 53/1788* 竹紙 *Bamboo paper*

Index

Bound in 1 t'ao   10 chuan   10 ts'e

Remarks

The University of Toronto Chinese Library
....

4

Accession No. 1623   Index No. 030-bbj3

Title 古今韻略 Ku Chin Yün Lüeh

Classification A-166

Subject

References

Author 清 邵長蘅纂 Compiled by Ch'ing, Shao Chang-Hêng

Edition 家藏精刻本 Private, family, fine-printed

毛邊紙 "Mao-Pien" paper

Index

Bound in 1 t'ao, 5 chuan, 5 ts'ê

Remarks

The University of Toronto Chinese Library

....

Accession No. *1624*   Index No. *120-25*

Title 律擕 *Lü Wei Chün*

Classification ヒ一137擕拷 雀侄 缘書

Subject *Collections of commentaries on the Classics*

References

Author *Written by* 清喬松年撰, *Ching, Chiao Sung-Nien*

Edition 强楚堂麻版, 光緒三年刻, 俘连低
Chiang-Shu-Tang edition, dated Kuang-Hsü 3/1877
black preserved
"Mien-Lien" paper

Index *a general table of contents for 14 chüan*

Bound in *1 t'ao, 14 chüan, 8 t'sê*

Remarks

516

The University of Toronto Chinese Library

....

Accession No. *1625*   Index No. *111 - cgic*

Title 和聖遺薪濟世殘屋 *Chih shêng Tao chai Tu shu Fu wei*

Classification 乙—13 9番分

Subject ✓ *miscellaneous writing of*
Philosophy and classics.

References

Author 明 彭元瑞 撰 *Written by* *Ming. Pêng Yüan-Juei*

Edition 明刻本，竹紙，大字 *large*
dated Ming period (1368-1643), Bamboo paper, big characters
block printed edition

Index *a general table of contents for chüan*

Bound in *1 t'ao, 2 chüan, 2 t'se*

Remarks

· ·

Accession No. 1626   Index No. 009-ee2a

Title 佛祖統系道景 Fo Tsu Tüng Hsi Tao Ching

Classification C-513

Subject

References

Author 明洪武間好道者繪 明清崇禎康熙咸豐光緒等年間編刻

Ming, Hung Wu Chien Hao Tao Chieh Chě Hui, Ming Ching Chung Chěn Kang Hsi Hsien Fěng

Edition 民國十年重印 First edition — During Ming + Ching Dynasty

Ming, Chung-Chěn period (1628-1643)

Ching, Köng-Hsi   " (1662-1722)

Hsien-Fěng   " (1851-1861)

Index   Kuang-Hsü   " (1875-1908)

Second edition — Ming-Kuo 10 Nien

                1921

Bound in   1 Tao   4 tsǔ

Remarks

518

. . . .

Accession No. 1627   Index No. 030-ゟ ʒ k n

Title 古文關鑑 Ku Wên Kuan Chien

Classification D-43 刻集一文

Subject

References

Author 呂祖謙 評 蔡文子 註, 徐樹屏考異
Commented by Lü Tsu-Chien (評), Tsai Wên-Tzu (註), Hsü Shu-Ping (考異)
         Annotated by
Edition

光緒戊戌, 江蘇書局刊版
dated Ching, Kuang-Hsü "Wu Hsü" /1898, Chiang-Su Book Company
                                              (printed)

Index A ge table of contents for 2 chüan

Bound in
      1 t'ao, 2 ts'ê, 2 chüan

Remarks

The University of Toronto Chinese Library

....

Accession No. /628   Index No. 072-0998

Title 曝書亭詞拾遺 Pao Shu Ting Tzu Shih I

Classification D — 118 詞曲, — 詞集,

Subject an individual collection of lyrics.

References

Author 清 朱彝尊撰, 翁之潤拾錄
Written by Ching, Chu I-Tsun (撰), Wêng Chih-Jun (拾錄) compiled.
Edition 常熟翁氏校刊, 綿連紙.
             'collated edition.
Cháng-Shu, Wêng-Shih recued, "Mien-Lien" paper

Index a general table of contents for 3 chüan.

Bound in / t'ao, 3 chüan, 1 ts'e

Remarks

520

The University of Toronto Chinese Library

. . . .

Accession No. *1629*   Index No. *040-寶綸堂*

Title 寶綸堂文鈔 *Pao Lun-Tang Wên Chao*

Classification *D-43*

Subject

References

Author 清 齋郘南蓍 *Ching, Chi Shao-Nan*

Edition 嘉慶年刊 *Dated, Chia-Ching period (1796-1820)*

Index

Bound in *1 t'ao   4 ts'ê*

Remarks

The University of Toronto Chinese Library

. . . .

Accession No. /630   Index No. 018-dck

Title 列仙傳 Lieh Hsien Chuan

Classification β—117 傳記

Subject collected biographies with pictures

References

Author 清, 還初道人輯。 compiled by Ch'ing, Huan-Chu-Tao-Jen

Edition 在茲堂刊 Tsai-Tzu-Tang edition block-engraving.

Index a general table of contents for 4 chüan

Bound in / t̆ao, 4 chüan, 2 tsê

Remarks

The University of Toronto Chinese Library

. . . .

Accession No. 1631   Index No. 164-cdcc

Title 刻雅齋丹黄小夏錄
Cho Ya Chai Tan Huang Hsiao Hsia Lu

Classification 乙-308 親西 一 韩文

Subject miscellaneous writings.

References

Author 清, 福增格撰. Written by Ching, Fu Tsêng-Ko

Edition 刻雅齋瀬车, 精寫刻车 乾隆辛巳年刊
綿連紙
Cho-Ya-Chai edition, fine printed edition
dated Chien-Lung "Hsin-Ssu"/1761.   "Mien-Lien" paper

Index none

Bound in 1 t'ao, 2 ts'ê

Remarks

523

Accession No. /632   Index No. 166-d c

Title 野記 Yeh Chi

Classification C-308 雜文

Subject miscellaneous writings

References

Author 明, 祝允明撰, *Written by* Ming, Chu Yün-Ming

Edition 元和祝氏藏板 同治甲戌年刊 毛邊紙 木無存
Yüan-Ho Chu-Shih edition, *block preserved* dated "Tung-Chih" "Chia-Hsü"/1874
"Tai-Shih" paper

Index none

Bound in / t'ao, 4 ch'üan, 2 ts'e

Remarks

The University of Toronto Chinese Library

. . . .

Accession No. 1633   Index No. 118-izbq

Title 篆文四書 Chuan Wên Ssŭ Shu

Classification A-131

Subject

References

Author 清 李光地等奉勅撰 Ching, Li Kuang Ti and others written by order

Edition 殿版 Palace ed.
白紙 White paper

Index

Bound in 2 函 10 tsê

Remarks

525

The University of Toronto Chinese Library

. . . .

Accession No. 1634   Index No. 074-bdch

Title 有明名賢遺翰 Yu Ming Ming Hsien I Han

Classification D-73-總集-文

Subject a general collection of prose

References

Compiled & block-engraved by

Author 清, 謝世伯精刻 Ching, Hsieh Shih-Po

Edition 漢泰文淵書局藕版, 咸豐之年刊, 綿連紙
Han Kao-Wên-Yüan Book Company, Hsien-Fêng 1/1851
preserved edition.
"Mien-Lien" Paper

Index a general table of contents for the 2 chüan

Bound in 1 t'ao, 2 chüan, 4 ts'ê

Remarks

526

....

Accession No. 1635   Index No. 140-m 3 b b

Title 薛文介公文集 Hsüeh Wên Chieh Kung Wên Chi

Classification 万

Subject

References

Author 明薛三省著 Ming, Hsueh San Sheng

Edition 明萬曆版 Ming, Wan Li blocks.

Index

Bound in 四卷二冊 4 Chuan, 2 Tsê

Remarks 竹紙 Bamboo Paper

虛白軒藏 Preserved in Hsii Po Hsüan

527

Accession No. 1636   Index No. 140-idfd

Title 董仲舒集 Tung chung shu chi

Classification X

Subject

References

Author 漢董仲舒著 Han, Tung Chung Shu

Edition 明刻本 Ming, Block-printing edition

Index

Bound in 一冊 1 Tsé

Remarks 竹紙 Bamboo Paper

528

The University of Toronto Chinese Library

....

Accession No. 1637   Index No. 060-hhbg

Title I.御製古稀說 I. yü chih Ku Hsi Shuo
　　II.附庫彭元瑞恭進頌九章 II. Fu Chên Pêng Yüan-Jui Kung chin Sung Chiu (chang)
Classification B-147 史部-載記

Subject

References

Author I. 乾隆帝 I. Chien-Lung Emperor
　　　　童語書 &Tung Kao. (書)
　　　　II. 彭元瑞恭 II. Pêng Yüan-Jui (恭)

Edition
　　大字　Big characters;
　　乾隆四十五年庚子　dated Chien-Lung 45 "Kêng-Tzŭ"/1780

Index
　　none

Bound in
　　1 táo, 1 tsê

Remarks

529

The University of Toronto Chinese Library

....

Accession No. 1638   Index No. 030-ba e7

Title 古本尚書 Ku Pên Shang Shu

Classification A-21

Subject

References

Author 元 金履祥表註 Annotated by Yüan, Chin Lü Hsiang Piao

Edition 掃葉山房映寫原本校刻本 Sao-Yeh-Shan-Fang manuscript from original ed & rivised.
光緒甲申年刻 綿連紙 "Mien-Lien" paper
Dated, Kuang-Hsü "Chia-Shen" 10/1884

Index

Bound in 1 t'ao   2 chuan   2 tsé

Remarks

530

The University of Toronto Chinese Library

....

Accession No. *1639*   Index No. *162-ils ps*

Title 道德寶章 *Tao Te Pao Chang*

Classification *C-511* 釋家

Subject

References

Author 宋道士白玉蟾註 *Annotated by Sung, Tao Shih, Pai Yü-Chán*
元趙松雪書 *Yüan, Chao Sung-Hsüeh*

Edition 京都白雲觀藏版 *Ching-Tu, Pai-Yün-Kuan edition*
宣紙 *"Hsüan" paper*

Index

Bound in *1 táo 1 tŝ*

Remarks

531

The University of Toronto Chinese Library

· ·

Accession No. *1690*   Index No. *075-idzl*

Title 楊忠烈遺集 *Yang Chung Lieh I Chi*

Classification

Subject

References

Author 明 楊漣著 *Ming, Yang Lien*
          Hupei, Ti-Erh-Chung-Hsüeh-Tang published

Edition 宣統二年 湖北第二中學堂印 用福州正誼書院本印行
          Dated, Hsuan-Tung "Kêng-Hsü" 2/1910

          Fu-Chou, Chêng-I-Shu-Yuan edition

Index

Bound in *1 t'ao. 2 ts'ǐ*

Remarks

Accession No. *1641*　　　　Index No. *106-ddcq*

Title 皇明北虜考 *Huang Ming Pei Lo Kao*

Classification *β—32* 紀事本末

Subject *complete historical narratives f*

References

Author 明，鄭曉撰 *Written by* *Ming, Chêng Hsiao*

Edition 明嘉靖十刊年 綿紙
Dated Ming, Chia-Ching *black engraved edition* *Period* *(1522-1566)*
"Mien-Lien" paper

Index *none*

Bound in *1 匣30, 1 帙2*

Remarks

The University of Toronto Chinese Library

. . . .

Accession No. *1142*   Index No. *061-eii*

Title 急就篇 *Chi Chiu Pien*

Classification *C —— 308* 雜家 - 雜文

Subject

References

Author 宋 王鹿麟 補注   毛也紙
Amended · Annotated by *Sung, Wang Ying-Lin*
Edition 蒲山王氏刊, 量天讓閣总藏, 又諸六年刊
Fu-Shan, Wang-Shih, printed edition, Tien-Jang-Ko home edition
dated Kuang-Hsü 6/1880. "Mao-Pien" paper

Index *None*

Bound in *1 t'ao, 4 chüan, 2 ts'e*

Remarks

534

The University of Toronto Chinese Library

· ·

Accession No. 1643   Index No. 149-j93d

Title 謝疊山先生詩註四種合刻
Hsieh Tieh Shan Hsien Shêng Hsiang Chu / Ssŭ Chung Ho Kô

Classification 姜赤 D-33 刊集 詩z
                    A-137 羣經總 x
Subject

References

                    Commented + Annotated by
Author 宋 謝枋得 評註 ∧ Sung, Hsieh Fang-Tê

Edition 清江樹昀梡刊年 光清九年刻, 綿連紙
        Ching, Chiang Shu-Yün ∧, Dated Kuang-Hsü 9/1883
                         revised edition
        "Mien-Lien" paper

Index

Bound in 1 Tâo, 15 Chüan, 4 Tsê

Remarks

The University of Toronto Chinese Library
....

Accession No. 1644   Index No. 030-hǎie

Title 問奇典註 Wen Chʻi Tien Chu

Classification C 348

Subject

References

Author 唐英增釋   Translated by:
Tang, Ying Tsēng

Edition 抄寫本 Manuscript

Index

Bound in 上下二冊 2 tʻċe

Remarks 竹紙 Bamboo Paper

The University of Toronto Chinese Library

. . . .

Accession No. *1646*   Index No. A *067-3239*

<u>Title</u> 文選音義 *Wên Hsüan Yin I*

<u>Classification</u>   *A - 166* 小學一韻書

<u>Subject</u>

<u>References</u>

                                    Compiled by
<u>Author</u> 清 余蕭客 輯著 *Ch'ing, Yü Hsiao-Ko*

<u>Edition</u>
          家藏版, 乾隆二十三年刻. 毛邊紙
Private family edition, dated Chien-Lung 23/1758, "Mao-Pien" paper

<u>Index</u> — *none*
      1 t'ao, 8 chüan, 4 tsê

<u>Bound in</u> ✓ ✓   ✓

<u>Remarks</u>

Accession No. 1647   Index No. 060—hjeg

Title 御纂性理精義 Yü Tsuan Hsing Li Chêng Yi

Classification C

Subject

References

Author 清李光地等奉敕撰 Ch'ing, Li Kuang Ti Written by order.

Edition 殿版 Palace edition

Index

Bound in 十一卷五冊 11 Chüan 5 Tsê

Remarks

The University of Toronto Chinese Library

. . . .

Accession No. 1648   Index No. 163-1c

Title 鄭志 Chêng Chih

Classification A—137 羣經總義

Subject a collection of commentaries on the Classics

References

Author 漢 鄭康成撰   綿連紙
Written by Han, chêng Káng chêng, "Mien-Lien" paper
Edition

Index a general table of contents for 3 chüan

Bound in 1 t/ao, 3 chüan, 3 tsê

Remarks

8

Accession No. 1649   Index No. 073-38

Title 書經 Shu Ching

Classification A-21

Subject

References

Author 宋 蔡沈集傳 Sung, Ts'ai Shen

Edition 湖北崇文書局版 Hupei, Chung-Wen Book Co.
同治七年刊 綿連紙 "Mien-Lien" paper
戊辰
Dated, Tung-Chih "Wu-Chen" 7/1868

Index

Bound in 1 t'ao   5 chuan   4 ts'e

Remarks

The University of Toronto Chinese Library

· ·

Accession No. 1650   Index No. 149-iedi

Title 諸佛世尊如來菩薩尊者名稱歌曲
Chu Fo Shih Tsun Ju Lai Yin Sa Tsun Chê Ming Chêng Ko Chü

Classification C-513

Subject

References

Author ·

Edition 明 永樂十五年印
Dated, Ming, Yung-Lo "Ting-Yu" 15/1417

Index

Bound in 1 t'ao   8 ts'ê

Remarks

33

Accession No. 1651   Index No. 162-33ke

Title 逆臣傳，貳臣傳 *Ni chên chuan, Êrh Chên Chuan*

Classification B-117

Subject

References

Author 清國史館原本 *Ching, Kuo Shih Kuan Yüan Pên Original copy*

Edition 羊松居士排字本 *Pan-Sung-Chü-Shih*
毛太紙 *"Mao-Tai" paper*

Index

Bound in 1 *t'ao*   8 *ts'ê*   16 *chuan*

Remarks

542

The University of Toronto Chinese Library
. . . .

Accession No. 1652   Index No. 015—2bhz

Title 冶古堂文集 Yeh Ku Tang Wên Chi

Classification 万

Subject

References

Author 清 呂履恆 著 Ch'ing, Lü Li Hêng

Edition 家藏版 Private-family printed edition.

Index

Bound in 五卷五册 5 Chüan 5 Tsê

Remarks 毛边纸 Mao-Pien Paper

The University of Toronto Chinese Library

. . . .

Accession No. 1653   Index No. 149.93⁻7

Title 誡子庸言 Chieh Tzǔ Yüng Yen

Classification C—13 德彛

Subject Family education & discipline

References

Author 清 葉仕替拜 Written by Ching, Mo Chi-chih

Edition 鈙印 板本 mulberry bark paper.
Chien
Type-setting edition, "pí" paper

Index None

Bound in 1 tào, 2 tsê

Remarks

544

The University of Toronto Chinese Library

....

Accession No. 1654   Index No. 120-9caj

Title 經字正蒙 Ching Tzŭ Chêng Mêng

Classification A - 137 161

Subject

References

Author 清 李文沂 篡 Compiled by Ching, Li Wên-Hsing

Edition 家藏版 Private family edition, Private Family Library, Kuang-Tung, Yang-Chêng-Ts'ui-Ching-Tang edition
光緒乙酉年刻 廣東羊土成萃經堂刻 毛邊紙 "Mao-Pien" paper

Index Dated, Kuang-Hsü "I-Gu" 11/1885

Bound in 1 Tao, 8 chuan, 8 ts'ê

Remarks

. . . .

Accession No. 1656   Index No. 085-乃夕

Title 淮南子 Huai Nan Tzŭ

Classification C-303

Subject

References

Author 漢 高誘注   清·莊達吉校刊(乾隆五十三年)
Han, Kao Yu   Ching, Chuang Ta Chi (revised)

Edition 光緒二年   浙江書局據莊氏本刊 Chê-Chiang Book co. published
丙子   according to Chuang-Shih ed.

Dated, Kuang-Hsü "Ping-Tzŭ" 2/1876

Index

Bound in 1 táo 6 tsin

Remarks

546

The University of Toronto Chinese Library
....

Accession No. 1657   Index No. 085-ㄥㄥㄨˇ

Title 清涼山新志、 *Ching Liang Shan Hsin Chih*

Classification B-207

Subject

References
          Ching, Kʻang-Hsi Emperor (*Chin-Ming-Tu-Li-Wu-Tai-Shen-Fan-Han-Ta-La-Ma-Lao-*
                                      Tsang-Tan-Pa (Shu-Hsü))
Author 清康熙 御製 (欽命督理五臺山蒼漢大喇嘛
                        老藏丹巴述序)

Edition 清康熙罳十年朔 朱圭恭鐫 *Chu Kuei-Kung*

        Dated, Ching, Kʻang-Hsi "Hsing-Ssŭ" 40/1701 May

Index

Bound in 1 tʻáo, 10 chüan, 4 tsʻê

Remarks

The University of Toronto Chinese Library

. . . .

.12

Accession No. 1658   Index No. 149-8988

Title 詩經音韻解 附龥解 Shih Ching Yin Yün Chieh
                          Fu Chü Chieh

Classification A-31

Subject

References

Author 清 甄士林音釋 ～ Translated by Ch'ing, Chên Shih-Lin

Edition 家藏版 精刻本 Private family ed. Home Library, Fine-printed edition
綿連紙   "Mien-lien" paper

Index

Bound in   5 chuan 5 ts'ê

Remarks

Accession No. 1659   Index No. 140-d388

Title 芥子園傳畫傳 Chieh Tzŭ Yüan Hua Chuan

Classification C-2²3

Subject

References

Author 宇內諸名家合訂　王槩摹古
J Yü-Nei Chou Ming Chia　Wang Chi
all famous authors

Edition

Index

Bound in 1 t'ao 4 ts'ê

Remarks

The University of Toronto Chinese Library

Accession No. /661   Index No. 085-93Ph
Title 浪跡叢談 Lang Chi Tsung Tan

Classification C—308 梁章鉅—梁七

Subject Miscellaneous writings of prose & poetry

References

Author 清梁章鉅撰, Written by Ching, Liang Chang-Chü

Edition 家藏板. 竹子紙
Private family Home Edition, Bamboo paper

Index a general table of contents for 11 chüan

Bound in 1 t/o, 11 chüan, 續 浪跡 8 chüan; 6 t'ai

Remarks

550

The University of Toronto Chinese Library

....

Accession No. *1662* .   Index No. *111-cbん*

Title 知 古 錄 *Chih Ku Lu*

Classification *C-33*

Subject

References

Author 清 毓孚 桓祫等纂輯。 *Compiled by Ching, Yü-fu, Hêng-Ling and others*

Edition 咸豐年刊 *Dated, Hsien-Fêng period (1851-1861)*

Index

Bound in *1 t'ao   3 ts'ê*

Remarks

The University of Toronto Chinese Library

· ·

119

Accession No. 1663   Index No. 075-cgg8

Title 李義山詩集箋註 Li I Shan Shih Chi Chien Chu

Classification ✓ D 38

Subject

References

Author 清 朱鶴齡原本　程夢星刪補
Ching, Chu Ho-Ling's Original copy Chên Mêng-Hsing revised

Edition 東柯草堂刊 Tang-Ko-Tsao-Tang
竹紙 夾板　bamboo paper, Wood-block

Index

Bound in 1 t'ao   3 chuan   8 ts'ê

Remarks

The University of Toronto Chinese Library
. . . .

Accession No. 1664   Index No. 109-M d f b
Title 瞿忠宣公集 Ch'ü chung Hsüan Kung Chi

Classification D

Subject

References

Author 明瞿式耜撰 Written by Ming, Chü Shih Szü
Edition 光緒丁亥重刊本
~~Redblock~~ Reprinted edition in Kuang-Hsü "Teng Hai" period.

Index

Bound in 十卷四冊 4 Chuan 4 Ts'e
Remarks 錦連紙 Mien-Lien Paper
夾版 ~~wooden block~~ wooden folder

The University of Toronto Chinese Library

．．．．．．．．．．．．．．．．．．．．．．．．．

Accession No. 1665   Index No. 030-bfj

Title 古詩源 Ku Shih Yuan

Classification 万

Subject

References

Author 清沈德潛選 Selected by Ch'ing, Shen Tê Ch'ien

Edition 思賢書局刊 Szu Hsien book co. block-engraving.

Index

Bound in 十四卷四册 14 Chuan 4 Ts'ê

Remarks 光緒年刻 Kuang-Hsü period.

錦連紙 Mien-Lien Paper

554

The University of Toronto Chinese Library

....

Accession No. *1666*   Index No. *118- e333*

Title 第一才子書 *Ti I Ts'ai Tzŭ Shu*

Classification *C-388*

Subject

References

Author 清 金聖嘆外書 毛宗崗評
Ching, Chin Shêng-Tan Wai-Shu Mao Tsung-Kang (commentary)

Edition 光緒三十三年 *丁未* 澹雅書局校刊 *Tan-Ya Book Co. rivised ed.*

Dated, Kuang-Hsü "Ting-Wei" 33/1907

Index

Bound in *2 t'áo 20 ts'á*

Remarks

The University of Toronto Chinese Library

....

Accession No. 1667   Index No. 162-ℓdkd

Title 選集漢印分韻 附續集二卷   Ch Hsüan Chi Han Yin fên Yün Fu Hsü Chi Êrh Chüan

Classification C-233

Subject

References Toronto No. 1205

Author 袁子三原本 謝雲生摹錄   Yüan Yü-San's ~~Yüan Pên~~ original copy Hsieh Yün-Shêng (copied)

Edition 清嘉慶二年 漱藝堂開雕 粵東省城 寶籍齋發兌   Sou-I-Tang Yüeh-Tung Capital, Pao-Chou-Chia Dated, Ching, Chia-Ching "Ting-Saŭ" 2/1797

Index

Bound in 1 t'ao   4 ts'ŏ

Remarks

556

The University of Toronto Chinese Library

....

Accession No. 1668　　　　　　　Index No. 060-*hh jj*

Title　御製日講四書解義　*Yü Chih Jih Chiang Ssü Shu Chieh I*

Classification　*A-131*

Subject

References

Author　清　喇沙里等奉勅纂　*Ching, La Sha and others Compiled by order.*

Edition　殿版 *Palace ed.*
　　　　毛邊紙 *"Mao-Pien" paper*

Index

Bound in　2 *t'ao*　8 *ts'ê*

Remarks

Accession No. *1669*　　　　　Index No. *171-20*

Title　隸續 *Li Hsü*

Classification　*B-107* 獨錄

Subject

References

Author　宋洪适撰。 *Written by Sung Hang Kúo*

Edition　日本浪華書林翻刻 *Japan, Lang-Hua-Shu-Lin printed*
　　　　文化紀元甲子梓 *dated Wên-Hua Chi Yuan "Chia-Tzŭ"*
　　　　竹紙, 夾板 *Bamboo paper, wooden folder*

Index

Bound in　*1 táo, 21 Chuan, 8 tsé*

Remarks

Accession No. 167 1   Index No. 149-033%

Title 讀律一得歌 Tu Lü I To Ko

Classification B-302

Subject

References

Author 古魯陽宗継增恒齋氏重編
Ku Lu Yang Tsung Chi Tsêng Hêng Chai Shih (re-edited)
Edition 光緒丁亥三月印
Dated, Kuang-Hsü "Ting-Hai" 13/1887 March

Index

Bound in 1 tao, 4 chuan, 4 ts'e

Remarks

559

The University of Toronto Chinese Library

....

Accession No. 1672   Index No. 075-i d i b

Title 楊忠愍公集 Yang Chung Min Kung Chi

Classification 万

Subject

References

Author 明楊繼盛撰 楊遠修原校
Written by Ming Yang Chi Sheng, Originally Collated by Yang Yuan Hsin
Edition 家藏板
private-family printed edition

Index

Bound in 六卷 五冊 附表忠記二卷
6 Chuan, 5 Ts'e
Remarks 同治年刻 Block-engraving in "Tung chih" period.
毛边紙 Miao Pien Paper
夾板 wooden folder

560

The University of Toronto Chinese Library

....

Accession No. 1673   Index No. HO—p363

Title 蘇長公小品 Su Chang Kung Hsiao pin

Classification δ

Subject

References

Author 明楊聖俞評選 *Commented & Selected by* Ming, Yang Sheng Yu

Edition 明刻本 Ming block-print edition

Index

Bound in 二卷二冊 2 Chuan, 2 Tse

Remarks 竹紙 Bamboo Paper
夾板 wooden block *wooden* for folder

Accession No. *1674*　　　　　Index No. *066-idjj*

Title 敬孚類稿 *Ching Fu Lei Kao*

Classification *D*

Subject

References

Author 清蕭穆撰 *Ching Hsiao Mu*

Edition 家藏版 *Private-printed edition.* (family)

Index

Bound in 十六卷八冊 *16 Chuan 8 Tse*

Remarks 光緒年刻
毛边紙 *Miao Pien Paper*
夾板 *wooden folder*

The University of Toronto Chinese Library

. . . .

23

Accession No. 1675   Index No. 030-bbdz

Title 古今列女傳 Ku Chin Lieh ɤ Nü Chuan

Classification β-117

Subject

References

Author 明 解學士撰 Written by ∧ Ming, Chieh Hsüeh-Shih

Edition 積香堂版 Chi-Hsin-Tang
嘉慶年刻 毛邊紙 "Mao-Pien" paper
Dated, Chia-Ching period (1796-1820)

Index

Bound in 1 tao, 4 ts'ǎ 4 chuen

Remarks

563

. . . .

Accession No. 1676   Index No. 170-mjm3

Title 隨園隨筆 Sui Yüan Sui Pi

Classification c-308

Subject

References

Author 袁枚著 Yüan Mei

Edition 清嘉慶戊辰年鐫   小倉山房藏板 block preserved.
~~Shan~~ ~~Tsang~~ Hsiao-Tsang-Shan-Fang ~~private~~ ~~printed~~
Dated, Ching, Chia-Ching "Wu-Chên" 13/1808

Index

Bound in 1 t'ao 6 ts'e

Remarks

564

Accession No. 1677   Index No. 8030-3m3d

Title 口鐸日鈔 K'ou To Jih Chao

Classification C-971

Subject

References

Author 明 西傳教士 思及艾 盤石慮口鐸 李九標筆記
Ming. Chinese Ch Ssu-Chi-Ai and Pan Lu   Li Chiu-Piao take notes.

Edition 1872 同治壬申十一年 上海慈母堂重梓 Shanghai, Tsu-Mu-Tang second ed.
Dated, Tung-Chih "Jên-Shen" 11/1872

Index

Bound in 1 t'áo 4 ts'ê

Remarks

. . . .

Accession No. *1678*　　　　　Index No. *102-gkci*

Title ~~書書合編~~ 畫傳合編 *Hua Chuan Ho Pien*

Classification *c-223*

Subject

References

Author 清王蘊菴著書　沈心友編 *Ching, Wang Yün-An and others Shen Hsin-Yu (edited)*

Edition 金閶書業堂重鐫珍藏　乾隆壬寅年 *Dated, Chien-Lung "Jen-Ying 47/1782 Ching-Chong-Shu-Yeh-Tong*

Index

Bound in *1 t'ao　4 ts'ê*

Remarks

Accession No. 1679   Index No. 057-2 m 2 j

Title 讲學錄類編 Chiang Hsüeh Lu Lei Pien

Classification C—318 雜家—雜文 (~~not~~)
                 Tsa Chia — Tsa Wên   (Miscellaneous writings)

Subject

References

Author 清,夏錫疇著 Ching, Hsia Hsi-Chou

Edition 仕學齋藏板 (道光十三年刊) 綿連紙印
         Shih-Hsüeh-Chia ~~edition~~ blocks preserved, dated Tao-Kuang 13/1833
         "Mien-Lien" paper

Index a general table of contents for 4 chüan

Bound in 1 t'ao, 4 chüan, 4 ts'ê

Remarks

567

The University of Toronto Chinese Library

....

Accession No. /680   Index No. 075-9ici

Title 梅瑞軒輯錄十種(卷上)
Mei Gui Hsüan Chi Lu Shih Chung I Shu

Classification 藝術 C338

Subject

References

Author 清. 茆泮林輯, Compiled by Ching. Mao Pan-Lin

Edition 梅瑞軒輯版 道光十四年刻, 綿連紙
Mei-Gui-Hsüan edition, block preserved, dated Tao-Kuang 14/1834
"Mien-Lien" paper

Index Different subject for each t'sè

Bound in / t'ao, 10 t'sè

Remarks

568

The University of Toronto Chinese Library

. . . .

13

Accession No. 1681   Index No. 072-dg

Title 易經 I Ching

Classification A-11

Subject

References

Author

Edition 江西書局刊 Chiang-Hsi Book Co. published
同治十三年刻 甲戌 綿連紙 夾板 "Mien-Lien" paper
Dated, Tung-Chih "Chia-Hsü" 13/1874

Index

Bound in 1 t'ao   4 chuan   2 ts'e

Remarks

The University of Toronto Chinese Library

....

Accession No. 1682   Index No. 077-ZZhd

Title 止止堂集 Chih chih Tang Chi

Classification C

Subject

References

Author 明戚武毅公著 Ming, Chi Wu J Kung

Edition 家藏版 Private-family printed edition

Index

Bound in 三卷四冊 3 Chüan, 4 Tsé

Remarks 錦連紙 Chien-Lien Paper
夾板 wooden folder

The University of Toronto Chinese Library
....

Accession No. 1683   Index No. 061-imia

Title 感應篇引經牋注 Kan Ying Pien Yin Ching Chien Chu

Classification c-731

Subject

References

Author 清 羅椒生升經 惠棟牋註 Annotated by Ching, Hui Tung 惠棟

Edition 同治年 羅惇衍及諸家輯刊 Compiled by Lo-Tun-Yen and others

        Dated, Tung-Chih period (1862-1874)

Index

Bound in 1 táo 1 tsér

Remarks

571

The University of Toronto Chinese Library

....

Accession No. 1684   Index No. 031-Lgge

Title 國語校注本三種 Kuo Yü Hsiao Chu Pên San Chung

Classification B-52

Subject

References

Author 清 汪遠孫 輯 Compiled by Ching. Wang Yüan-Sun

Edition 振綺堂汪氏刊本 Chên-Chi-Tang, Wang-Shih black print ed.

道光丙午年刻　綿連紙 "Mien-Lien" paper
Dated, Tao-Kuang "Ping-Wu" 26/1846

Index

Bound in 1 t'ao   6 ts'ê

Remarks

Accession No. *1685*   Index No. *037-azjc*

Title 太谷縣志, *T'ai Ku Hsien Chih*

Classification *B-194*

Subject

References

Author 清 張曾諲等奉勅修 *ching, Chang I and others Amended by order*

Edition 官版 *official copy*
乾隆六十年刊 *Dated, Chien-Lung "Ting-Mao" 60/1795*
丁卯

Index

Bound in / *T'ao* 9 *Chuan* 8 *Ts'a*

Remarks

Accession No. 1686   Index No. 015-hzgh

Title 淨土聖賢錄 Ching Tu Shêng Hsien Lu

Classification C-513

Subject

References

Author 清 彭際清編 (乾隆四十八年)
edited by Ching, Pêng Chi-ching
Edition 嘉慶庚午年年刊 Dated, Chia-Ching "Kêng-Wu" 15/1810

Index

Bound in 1 Táo 3 tsʻ

Remarks

574

The University of Toronto Chinese Library

....

Accession No. 1687   Index No. 170-33c

Title 陋巷志 Lou Hsiang Chih

Classification B—194 地理 — 別志
                   Ti ti   Pieh-Chih

Subject Local gazeteer. with picture & commentary

References

Author 明. 呂兆祥重修 Ming. Lü Chao-Hsiang revised edition

Edition 明嘉靖版 Dated Ming. Chai Chia-Ching period (1522-1566)

Index a general table of contents for 8 chüan

Bound in / tao. 4 tse. 8 chüan

Remarks

The University of Toronto Chinese Library

. . . .

11

Accession No. *1688*   Index No. *012-bgk*

Title 六經圖 *Liu Ching Tú*

Classification *A-173*

Subject

References

Author 清 鄭之僑編輯 *edited o compiled by* *Ching, Chêng Chih-Chiao*

Edition 述堂藏板 精刻本 *Shu-Tang* *blocks preserved edition* *private printed*
綿連紙 *"Mien-lien" paper*

Index

Bound in *2 T'ao* *12 ts'e*

Remarks

576

The University of Toronto Chinese Library
....

Accession No. 1689   Index No. 030-bCzz

Title 台州金石錄 Tai Chou Chin Shih Lu

Classification B

Subject

References

Author 清黃瑞編輯。 Compiled by Ch'ing, Huang Shui

Edition 吳興嘉業堂刊
Wu Hsing Chia Yeh Tang Block-printing edition

Index

Bound in 十三卷 台甎五卷 闕訪四卷 八冊
13 chüan

Remarks 竹紙
Bamboo Paper

. . . .

12

Accession No. 1690   Index No. 149-____

Title 詩經講意鐸振 Shih Ching Chiang I To Chên

Classification A-31

Subject

References

Author 清 江環輯著   徐奮鵬刪補
Compiled by Ching, Chiang Huan   Hsü Fên-Fu (revised)
Edition 梅墅石渠閣刊 Mei-Shu-Shih-Chü-Ko
竹紙 bamboo paper

Index

Bound in 1 t'ao   8 chuan   8 ts'ê

Remarks

The University of Toronto Chinese Library

. . . .

Accession No. *1691*　　　　Index No. *064-ml2*

Title 擇施錄 *Tsê Shih Lu*

Classification *C — 308 部分 一 部大*

Subject *miscellaneous writings of philosophy.*

References

　　　　　　　　　　Compiled by

Author 清, 方令吉无 *Ching, Fang-Chin-Wu-Shih*

Edition 官版, 利陸五十八年刻, 綿連紙
Official printed edition, Chien Lung 58/1793, "Mien-Lien" paper
　　　　　　　　　　　　dated

Index *a general table of contents for 9 Chüan*

Bound in *1 t'ao, 9 Chüan, 4 Tsê*

Remarks

The University of Toronto Chinese Library

· ·

Accession No. *1692*   Index No. *118-2mP3*

Title 笠澤叢書 *Li Tsê Tsung Shu*

Classification 刀—33—別集—詩文 *(Individual collection—*
pieh chi   shih wên   Poetry and prose)

Subject *An individual collection of poetry & prose*

References

Author 唐，陸龜蒙撰 *written by* *Táng, Lu Kuei-Mêng*

Edition 汲藏版，雍正李字刊. 枌紙代，木板
Private ~~family~~ *edition, "Fên" paper "dated Yüng-Chên period (1723-1735)*
Wood block

Index *a general table of contents for 4 tsê*

Bound in / *tao, 4 tsê*

Remarks

580

The University of Toronto Chinese Library
....

Accession No. 1693   Index No. 031-6Xde

Title 四書集註 Ssǔ Shu Chi Chu

Classification A-131

Subject

References

Author

Edition 李氏珍藏·大字精刻本 Li-Shih privated ed. Fine-printed in big letters 金陵狀元閣印 白毛邊紙 White "Mao-Pien" paper

Index

Bound in 1 Tao, 4 ts'ê

Remarks

581

The University of Toronto Chinese Library

. . . .

Accession No. ~~1694~~ 1694   Index No. 128 - g i k 8

Title 聖諭像解 Shêng Yü Hsiang Chieh

Classification C-13

Subject

References

Author 清 梁延年著(康熙二十年)   恩壽重梓(光緒二十八年)
        Ching, Liang Yen-Nien   Ên Shou (revised)
Edition 光緒二十九年重刊 倣照石印 Fang Chao lithographic edition
        癸卯

        Dated, Kuang-Hsü "Kuei-Mao" 29/1903

Index

Bound in 1 t'ao   9 tsê

Remarks

582

The University of Toronto Chinese Library

. . . .

Accession No. *1695-A*   Index No. *007-gdhg*

Title 二希堂文集 *Erh Hsi Tang Wên Chi*

Classification *D-43*

Subject

References *Toronto No. 506*

Author 清 蔡世遠著 *Ching, Tsai Shih-Yüan*
Min-Chong-To-I Chai # privat-printed

Edition 光緒二十五年重刊 己亥 閩漳多藝齋藏板
Dated, Kuang-Hsü "Chi-Hai" 25/1899

Index

Bound in *1 táo   6 tsê*

Remarks

Accession No. *1696*   Index No. *030-bbch*

Title 右台仙館筆記 *Yu Tai Hsien Kuan Pi Chi*

Classification 乙一318 雜文

Subject *miscellaneous writings*

References

Author 清，俞樾著 *Ching, Yü Yüeh*

Edition 家藏版，綿連紙，木板

private family edition, "Mien-Lien" paper, wood folder

Index *none*

Bound in *1 t'ao, 16 chüan. 6 t'sê*

Remarks

The University of Toronto Chinese Library
....

Accession No. *1697*   Index No. *042-3b*

Title 小 四 書 *Hsiao Ssŭ Shu*

Classification *C-13*

Subject

References

Author 清 陸稼書先生校訂 *Ch'ing, Lu Chia Shu Hsien Shêng (revised)*

Edition 康熙癸酉年　鋤經閣重刊 *Ch'u-Ching-Ko reprinted edition*

Dated, *K'ang-Hsi "Kuei-Yu" 32/1693*

Index

Bound in *1 t'ao   4 tsê*

Remarks

. . . .

Accession No. *1698*   Index No. *070-3392*

Title 方言疏証 *Fang Yen Su Chêng*

Classification 乙—308 雜家——雜文
                          Tsa Chia — Tsa Wên

Subject *Miscellaneous writings about dialect with commentary.*

References

Author 清, 戴震疏証 *take note by* *Ching, Tai Chêng-Su*

Edition 漢京精重刊, ↑[?]清謝[?]車, 光緒手刻, 竹紙
Han Ching-I revised
Wei-Po-Hsieh's edition, *Dated* ↑ *Kuang-Hsü period (1875-1908)*
Bamboo paper

Index *none*

Bound in *1 t'ao, 13 Chüan, 4 ts'ê*

Remarks

The University of Toronto Chinese Library

. . . .

Accession No. *11* 1699   Index No. 075-7ch

Title 校字錄 Hsiao Tzu Lu

Classification A

Subject

References

Author 清 史評等撰 *Written by* Ching, Shih Ping and others

Edition 中箱本 Pocket-edition

道光七年刊 毛邊紙 "Mao-Pien" paper
J Hsuan   Dated, Tao-Kuang "Ting-Hai" 7/1827

Index

Bound in 1 T'ao 2 ts'e

Remarks

The University of Toronto Chinese Library

....

Accession No. 1700   Index No. 140-m z h b

Title 薛文清公集 Hsüeh Wên-ch'ing Kung Chi

Classification D

Subject

References

Author 明薛瑄撰 *Written by* Ming, Hsüeh Hsüan

Edition 家藏版 Private *family* Printed edition

Index

Bound in 四册   4 Ts'e

Remarks 共四種

毛太紙 Mao Tai Paper

The University of Toronto Chinese Library

. . . .

Accession No. *1701*　　　　Index No. *102-93-23*

Title 鐵山先生淨注四種 *Tieh Shan Sh Hsien Shêng Ping Cha Ssŭ Chung*

Classification C-n D> 叢書 D-33 別集 詩文

Subject D-33 別集一詩文 A-137 羣經總义

References

Author 宋、謝枋得淨注 *Commented & annotated by* (Sung) Hsieh Fang-Tê

Edition 汪氏精刊本 同治辛未年刊, 綿連紙 *Wang-Shih fine printed edition, dated Tung-Chih "Hsin-Wei" /1871 "Mien-Lien" paper*

Index

Bound in 1 t'ao, 4 ts'ê

Remarks

The University of Toronto Chinese Library

. . . .

Accession No. 1702   Index No. 085-ke

Title 漢傍 Han Chün

Classification と—308 華文

Subject *Miscellaneous writing of Han*

References

Compiled by
Author 明,林銳 解 (Ming) Lin Yüeh

Edition 明,萬曆 林, 毛太 紙七
Ming, Wan-li edition, "Mao-Tai" paper

Index *a general table of contents for 10 chüan*

Bound in *1 t'ao, 10 chüan, 4 t'sê*

Remarks

The University of Toronto Chinese Library

. . . .

Accession No. 1703   Index No. 149-0332

Title 讀律一得歌 Tu Lü I Ko Tê Ko

Classification B-302

Subject

References

Author 古魯陽宗継增恆齋氏重編 Ku Lu Yang Tsung Chi Tsêng Hêng
                                    Chai Shih (revised)

Edition 光緒丁亥三月印
        Dated — Kuang-Hsü "Ting-Hai" 13/1887

Index

Bound in 1 tao, 4 chuan, 4 ts'ê

Remarks

The University of Toronto Chinese Library

....

Accession No. 1704   Index No. 028-clcz

Title 去偽齋文集 Chü Wei Chai Wên Chi

Classification D-43

Subject

References

Author 明 呂坤著 (Ming.) Lü Kúng

Edition 萬曆年間刊 曹琛應菊藏板

Dated,—Wan-Li period 1593-1619

Index

Bound in 1 tʻao   10 tsʻé

Remarks

592

√x

The University of Toronto Chinese Library

....

6

Accession No. 1705   Index No. 179-3gdk

Title 詩經集傳音釋 Shih Ching Chi Chuan Yin Shih

Classification A-31

Subject

References

Author 宋朱熹集傳 清許謙名音釋 (Sung), Chu Hsi; (Ching) Hsü Chian-Ming (commentary)

Edition 家藏版 Private-printed family edition.
毛邊紙 求板 "Mao-Pien" paper
                     Wood-block

Index

Bound in 1 tao, 20 chuan, 4 ts'e

Remarks

Accession No. 1706   Index No. 031-bdb3

Title 四書朱子本義匯叅 Ssŭ Shu Chu Tzŭ Pên I Hui Tsan

Classification A-136

Subject

References

Author 清 王步青輯 *Compiled by* (Ching) Wang Pu-ching

Edition 敦復堂藏版 Tun-Fu-Tang *block preserved ed.* *private printed*
江蘇學院頒行 毛太紙 "Mao-Tai" paper
Chiang-Su-Hsüeh-Yuan

Index

Bound in 5 t'ao, 14 chüan, 47 ts'ê

Remarks

The University of Toronto Chinese Library

.... 146-3909
                           075-9909
                           085-9dhb

Accession No. 1707 12 chüan   Index No. 12 chüan Hai Tung I Shih 18 chüan
         Hsi Nan Chi Shih 2 tse   Tung Nan Chi Shih 2 tse   1 tse

Title 西南紀事 12卷 東南紀事 12卷 海東逸史 18卷
         2 册   2 册   1 册

Classification B一32 紀事写末

Subject complete historical narratives of south-west
south-east and east part of the China

References

Author 清. 邵廷采撰, Written by (Ching) Shao Ting T'sai.

Edition 即邵氏刊年 毛边纸
                    Printed-
         Shao-Wu, Hsü-Shih, edition, "Mao-Pien" paper

Index a general table of contents for each book.
       西南紀事 2 tse, 東南紀事 2 tse, 海東逸史 1 tse.
       Hsi Nan Chi Shih   Tung Nan Chi Shih   Hai Tung I Shih
Bound in 1 tao, 42 chüan, 5 tse

Remarks

Accession No. 1708   Index No. 106—зd зd

Title 白沙子全集 pai sha Tzu ch'üan chi

Classification Ò

Subject

References

Author 明陳獻章著 (Ming), Ch'ên Hsien Chang

Edition 碧玉樓藏版
Pi Yü Lou block preserved edition

Index

Bound in 十三卷十冊 13 Chüan 10 Ts'e

Remarks 乾隆辛卯重刊本 Reprinted edition in ch'ien-lung "Hsin Maõ"
綿連紙 Mien-Lien Paper

596

The University of Toronto Chinese Library

. . . .

69

Accession No. *1709*   Index No. *072-del gh*

Title 明 季 遺 聞 *Ming Chi I Wên*

Classification *B-52*

Subject

References

Author 清 鄒 漪 輯 *Compiled by* *(Ching) Tsou I*

Edition 家藏版 *Private-printed family edition.*

順治年刻 綿紙 夾板 *"Mien" paper, Wood-block*

Index *Dated — Shun-Chih period 1644-1661*

Bound in *1 t'ao   4 chuan   4 ts'ə*

Remarks

597

. . . .

Accession No. *1710*   Index No. *085—庋 e 3*

Title 浮邱子 *Fou Ch'iu Tzu*

Classification *C*

Subject

References

Author 清 湯海秋 著 (*Ch'ing*) *T'ang Hai Chiu*

Edition 家藏版 *Private - family printed edition.*

Index

Bound in 十二卷 四冊 *12 Chuan 4 Ts'e*

Remarks 竹紙 *Bamboo Paper*

The University of Toronto Chinese Library

. . . .

Accession No. 1711   Index No. 169-k39c

Title 關帝寶訓 Kuan Ti Pao Hsün

Classification c-368

Subject

References

Author

Edition 雍清 雍正辛亥歲鐫
Dated — Ching, Yung-Chêng "Hsin-Hai" 9/1731

Index

Bound in 1 t'ao   4 ts'ǔ

Remarks

The University of Toronto Chinese Library

....

Accession No. 1713   Index No. 040-c d h d

Title 安雅堂集 An Ya Tang Chi

Classification 万

Subject)

References

Author 清宋琬著 (Ching) Sung Wan

Edition 家藏版 Private-printed family edition

Index

Bound in 六種計共十六冊

Remarks 康熙年刻 block engraving in "Kang-Hsi" Period
毛边紙 Mao Pien Paper
夾板 wooden block

600

The University of Toronto Chinese Library
....

Accession No. 1714   Index No. 075-ik 93

Title 楹聯叢話 Ying Lien Tsung Hua

Classification D-63   總集-詩文

Subject

References

Author 福州, 梁章鉅 (Fu-chou) Liang Chang-Chü

Edition 道光庚子春 dated Tao-Kuang "Kêng Tzǔ" Spring /1840
環碧軒藏版 Huan-Pi-Hsüan block Preserved edition

Index none   1 tao, 8 chüan, 8 tsê

Bound in ✓ ✓ ✓

Remarks

Accession No. 1715   Index No. 106-ぁ九ヲキ

Title 皇朝文典 *Huang cháo Wên Tien*

Classification 刀

Subject

References

Author 清李兆洛重鰲次 (Ching), *Li chao Lê, Chung Li Tžǔ*

Edition 李澄校刊本
Li Chên. Collated edition

Index

Bound in 七十六卷 十六冊
76 Chuan, 16 Tsê

Remarks 竹紙 *Bamboo Paper*

6

Accession No. 1717   Index No. 113-mcd

Title 禮記省度 Li Chi Shêng Tu

Classification

Subject

References

Author 清 彭頤纂 (Ching) Pêng I, Compiled by

Edition 家藏版 Private-printed family edition
白竹紙 嘉慶年刻 White bamboo paper
Dated — Chia-Ching period 1796—1820

Index

Bound in 1 tao, 4 chuan, 4 tsê

Remarks

The University of Toronto Chinese Library

. . . .

Accession No. 1718   Index No. 002-CCim

Title 中州道學編 Chung Chou Tao Hsüeh Pien

Classification C — 13 道學

Subject a general collection of famous scholars & philosophers in "Sung", "Ming" + "Ching" dynasty.

References

Author 清, 耿介 輯 compiled by (Ching), Kêng Chieh

Edition 嵩陽書院藏版 綿連紙 block preserved
Sung-Yang-Shu Yüan edition, "Mien-Lien" paper

Index

Bound in / 套, 2 函, 4 冊

Remarks

604

The University of Toronto Chinese Library

....

Accession No. *1719*   Index No. *012-bh33*

Title 六朝文絜 *Liu Cháo Wên Chieh*

Classification *D—63* 総集一诗文

Subject *A general literary collection of prose and poetry; with commentary.*

References

Author 清 许槤評選 朱鈴校
Selected by (Ching) Hsü Lien (選) Collated by Chu Chün (校) 已卯

Edition 欽光绪己卯 先清 朱氏本刊, 绵連紙 木板
Commentaries printed in red, dated Kuang-Hsü "己卯" /1879
"Mien-Lien" paper, wood block.   Chi

Index *A detail table of contents for*

Bound in *1 tào, 4 chüan, 4 tsê*

Remarks

The University of Toronto Chinese Library

. . . .

Accession No. 1720   Index No. 170-iddz

Title 陽明先生集要三編 Yang Ming Hsien Shêng Chi Yao San Pien

Classification D-33

Subject

References

Author 明 施四明評輯王守仁著作 (Ming,) Shih Ssŭ-Ming; (annotations) Wang Jen Shoueˌjen

Edition 光緒己卯年重刊 板存貴州省城外扶風山陽明祠 Kuei-chow, Fu-Fung-Shan, Yang-Ming-Shih Dated — Kuang-Hsü "己卯-Mao" 5/1879 Chi

Index

Bound in 2 t'áo 12 ts'é

Remarks

The University of Toronto Chinese Library

. . . .

40

Accession No. 1721   Index No. 072-dq

Title 明鑑 Ming Chien

Classification B-12

Subject

References

Author 清 胡敬等纂 Compiled by (Ching) Hu Ching and others

Edition 官版 Official ed.
嘉慶年刻　白紙 White paper
Dated — Chia-Ching period 1796-1820

Index

Bound in 1 t'ao   24 chuan   12 ts'ê

Remarks

The University of Toronto Chinese Library

．．．．．．．．．．．．．．．．．．．．．．．

Accession No. 1722   Index No. 030-&bge

Title 史通註 Shih Tung Chu

Classification B-367

Subject

References

Author 唐 劉子玄撰著　明 陳繼儒訂註

Written by
Edition Táng, Liü Tzŭ Hsüan. (Ming.)Chén chi-ju (commentate)(hounded & annotated)

Index

Bound in 1 tào   6 tsè

Remarks

Accession No. 1724   Index No. 060-hh39

Title 御製文餘集 yü chih Wên yü chi

Classification D-23

Subject

References

Author 清 乾隆帝書(Ching.) Chien Lung Emperor

Edition 殿板 Palace ed.
(版)

Index

Bound in 1 tao 2 tsê

Remarks

The University of Toronto Chinese Library
. . . .

Accession No. 1725   Index No. 085-1213

Title 溫飛卿詩集箋注 Wên Fei Ching Shih Chi Chien Chu

Classification D—38 別集—詩

Subject As individual collection of poetry with commentary.

References

Author 唐, 溫庭筠撰, 清, 曾益等箋注
Written by (Táng), Wên Ting-Yün 撰 (Ching) Tsêng I-Chien (原注) Originally annotated

Edition 萬卷山房刊, 秀野草堂版
Wan-Chou-Shan-Fang edition, Hsiu-Yeh-Tsao-Táng edition

Index A general table of contents for 9 chüan

Bound in 1 tào, 4 tsê, 9 chüan

Remarks

610

The University of Toronto Chinese Library

....

Accession No. 1726 Index No. 140. *i k r j*

Title 萬壽衢歌樂章 *Wan Shou Chü Ko Yüeh Chang*

Classification C-228

Subject

References

Author 清 彭元瑞集乾隆御製詩句 (Ching) *Pêng Yüan-Jui with collected*
2.
1. *Chien Lung Emperor's Poems*

Edition 乾隆五十五年刊 *Dated — Chien-Lung "Kêng-Hsü" 55/1790*
庚戌

Index

Bound in 1 *t'ao* 4 *ts'ê*

Remarks

The University of Toronto Chinese Library

. . . .

Accession No. *1727*　　　Index No. *031-c ʒ i d*

Title 回文類集 *Hui Wên Lei Chi*

Classification *D—63* 詩集一詩文

Subject *a general collection of a special sort of*
poetry with commentaries & pictures & ~~symbol~~

References

Author 清, 桑世昌纂輯 *Compiled in Order by* (*Ching*) *Sang Shih-Chāng*

Edition *✻*麟華玉堂藏板 *like preserved* 連史紙
Lin-Yü-Tang edition, "Lien-Shih" paper

Index *a general table of contents for 10 chüan*

Bound in *1 t'ao, 10 chüan, 4 ts'ê*

Remarks

The University of Toronto Chinese Library

. . . .

Accession No. 1728   Index No. 085-bj 齋 Chai

Title 求闕齋日記類鈔 Ch'iu ch'üeh ~~Chi~~ jih chi Lei
ch'ao

Classification D

Subject

References

Author 清曾國藩隨筆王啟原校編
Written by (Ch'ing) Tseng Kuo Fan, Collated & edited by Wong Chi Yuan.
Edition 傳忠書局刊   edition.
Ch'uan Chung book company Block-printing.

Index

Bound in 上下二冊 2 tse

Remarks 光緒二年刻 block engraving in the 2nd year of Kuang Hsü.
毛邊紙 Mao-Pien Paper

613

. . . .

8

Accession No. *1729*　　　　　　Index No. *113-mcgl*

Title 禮記通識 *Li Chi Tung Shih*

Classification *A-56*

Subject

References

Author 巖尹茵城著 *Yen Yin gui chêng*

Edition 茵惇叙堂刊　宣統辛亥年刻
竹紙 夾版 *Bamboo paper, Wood-block*
Dated — Hsüan-Tung "Hsin-Hai" 3/1911

Index

Bound in *1 tao, 4 chuan, 4 tse*

Remarks

The University of Toronto Chinese Library

. . . .

Accession No. 1730   Index No. 199-Lg L 3

Title 論語淺解 *Lun Yü Chien Chieh*

Classification A-134

Subject

References

Author 清 喬松年註 (*Ching*) Chiao Sung-Nien *Annotated by*

Edition 強恕堂藏版 Chiao Shu Tang *block preserved.*
光緒三年刻 綿連紙 夾板 "*Mien-lien*" *paper*
Dated — Kuang-Hsü "Ting-chou" *Wood-block* 3/1877

Index

Bound in 1 *t'ao* 4 *chuan*, 4 *ts'e*

Remarks

615

Accession No. *1731*   Index No. *149-李章书*

Title 渴子随笔印钞. *K'o Tzŭ Sui Pi Chieh Lu*

Classification *C-308 韩文*

Subject *collection from the 70 authors of homiletical writings*

References

Author 懒判 张义梁群 *Compiled by* (*I-Fêng*), *Chang Yu-Chü*

Edition 家群版
private family home edition

Index *a general table of contents for 6 chüan*

Bound in *1 t'ao, 6 ts'ê, 6 chüan*

Remarks